Tree Spirits

&

Wood Wisdom

Thomas Lee Freese

Stellium Books
Grant Park, Illinois 60940

Cover Art by Annette Munnich

Tree Spirits and Wood Wisdom's images appear courtesy of the author.

Tree and open field Creacy Mahan Nature Preserve, KY photo by Thomas Freese

Medical Disclaimer

The information in this book is not intended or implied to be a substitute for professional medical advice, diagnosis or treatment. All content, including text, graphics, images and information, contained on or available through this book is for general information purposes only. The author and publisher make no representation and assumes no responsibility for the accuracy of information contained on or available through this book, and such information is subject to change without notice. You are encouraged to confirm any information obtained from or through this book with other sources and review all information regarding any medical condition or treatment with your physician.

NEVER DISREGARD PROFESSIONAL MEDICAL ADVICE OR DELAY SEEKING MEDICAL TREATMENT BECAUSE OF SOMETHING YOU HAVE READ IN THIS BOOK.

This book does not recommend, endorse or make any representation about the efficacy, appropriateness or suitability of any specific tests, products, procedures, treatments, services, opinions, health care providers or other information that may be contained on or available through this book.

Table of Contents

Acknowledgments

I want to thank all those who appreciate and have over time appreciated my artwork, including those pieces crafted in wood. I am grateful for all the patrons who have purchased my wood jewelry, spoons, ornaments and wands. I would like to thank Camille Moritz and also Skipper who drew my attention to the possibility of making wands. I'd like to return appreciation to all those who contributed to the material for this book, particularly those who wrote testimonials and also to my three psychic friends—Angie Clark, Laura Berlin and Dale Epley. Thanks to those folks who have brought me wood pieces that I had not yet worked with, whether gift or trade, including Larry Trout, Bill Freese, Barbara Magruder, Lindsay Frost, Betty Buehler, Robert Tuemler, Roberta and Lonnie Brown, Alan Mason, Sharon Cassel, Melvin Ollhoff, Judy Bagan, Dan Vandolah, Chau, the Roaches, David Kempf, Don and Marilynn Spitz, Jan Hunter, Nanci Wesling, Becky and Pat Henry, Patrice Will Ising, Tom Bishop, Margie Beatty, Frank Lyne, Warren May, Rodney of Santa Fe. Thanks for photographs by Angela Hurd and picture digital processing by Dale Greer. I'm grateful for Beth Wilder's stories, artwork, photos and review. Also kudos several online sources that provided meanings for the woods that I didn't have samples (and thus was not able to send to the collaborating psychics); these were Kate Raymond and Fey Wilde & Gina Salvatoriello. And a heartfelt thanks to Llewellyn Worldwide for their permission to include one of my very favorite stories.

My gratitude also goes to all those who have written about trees in nonfiction and fiction, in stories for children and adults. And thanks to those who have shared about their healing and spiritual experiences with trees.

"Paper flower

Paper bird

Paper moon

Who walks

The wild earth

Any more?"

Paul Reps, "Zen Telegrams"

Introduction

Trees are our companions. If you understand that statement then you will be open to the wisdom offered in this book. If you don't understand that statement, on whichever level or levels, then you may not be ready for the information shared in the following pages. In the Gospel of Mark (4:9) it is written "Then Jesus said, "He who has ears to hear, let him hear."

I understand that not everyone walks the journey of an intuitive, a sensitive one. Although that is my path, I have met many who comprehend the power and wisdom, the feeling of being around trees. And that feeling is oftentimes a good one. Have you not, and perhaps you even now have a favorite tree? When you were upset, sad and needed emotional release, did you go outside to your yard, to visit your trees there, or in the woods, in a park? Have you stood before a tree that seems to so arrest your attention that you want to hear it speak, to find its voice, to commune with its wise longevity?

Ancient Ash tree and chair swing, photo by Thomas Freese

Trees are our ancient companions and they were here long before us. Yes, trees have a spirit and a consciousness and you can communicate with trees. Even a piece of the tree contains the whole of the tree; each bit of bark, or root, or branch or leaf or seed or fruit offers the essence of the wisdom and healing energies for that tree. A wood crafted item not only is a portal to the power of that tree but also adds the positive loving energy of the artist. Trees accompany us in the ways of our life from wooden cradle to wood coffin. They give us oxygen to breathe and take our carbon dioxide waste. Trees hold the land and draw the very rains that we desperately need to replenish and nourish our environment. Trees store carbon and yet when left to their natural cycle, release it in a beneficial and time extended manner.

Fractal pattern underneath shed away bark, juniper wood, photo by Thomas Freese

Trees offer the methods for physical healing through flower essences, bark for headaches, root for cleansing tonics, and much more. Yet trees also are willing to share companionship, shade, shelter, and a thousand and one practical items made from wood. Listen to a classical concert or folk guitar and you know the vibration of wood put forth in guitar and violin. From hardwood floors to sturdy house timbers to wooden ships, can you imagine a civilization without trees?

Trees are affected by the great cycles of our planet and the subtle yet real energies coming from our solar system and beyond. Trees absorb all that happens in their life, as humans, and they show in their trunk and tree rings the trauma of past years or centuries. You can study dendritic rings to discover ancient years of drought or cycles of good rains, or see where forest fires have ravaged the land. That trees live longer lives than we humans is well established. So why not seek the wisdom of a being that has been here for 100 or 1,000 or 5,000 years? I have stood before trees of great age, such as the Veteran Oak in Lexington, Kentucky and the amazing ancient Sassafras in Owensboro, also in Kentucky. I call these gentle but strong giants "Legacy" trees.

Have you planted or transplanted a tree? Have you lived long enough to witness a tree mature and become old...like you? There are stories of people who have changed a deserted and forsaken landscape into thriving woodland, through the efforts of their own heart and hands, planting one tree at a time. Over time, trees can migrate hundreds of miles, assisted by birds, wind and water. Studies have shown that trees can share nutrients and water with other trees, through their roots.

We humans often project positive or negative traits onto trees. There are trees in some towns that were used for hanging, and due to no fault of those trees they are nevertheless seen a suspicious eye—perhaps we project our guilt onto that tree? Some trees appear to have faces or the trunk and branch form a certain animal. I have seen the Donkey Tree, not far from Springfield, Kentucky. Teenagers have built up a crazy folklore about that tree, and it has its own online page.

The Donkey Tree photo by Thomas Freese

The Witches' Tree in Old Louisville has a
wonderful history ascribed to it and is included in one of
the local ghost tours. Many folks love to visit the Witches'
Tree and leave offerings on its trunk. Here below is a
condensed version from "True Ghost Stories and Eerie
Legends from America's Most Haunted Neighborhood" by
David Domine, with the story told from the tree's point of
view:

"I am the Witches' Tree. Back in the day, I was a tall, perfectly straight maple tree. I was the favorite meeting spot for a coven of local witches, who would meet at night under my branches and cast their spells and brew their potions.

But this all changed in 1889 when the city of Louisville announced plans to chop me down for the next year's May Day festivities. May Day is something that isn't celebrated much in this country anymore, but in Victorian times, this was a popular celebration, and the centerpiece of any May Day festivities was the tall, straight tree that was stripped of its bark and then festooned with garlands and greenery as the Maypole. Of course when the witches found out about the new plans for me, their beloved tree, they weren't pleased and they warned the organizers not to fell me.

Alas, they didn't really take witches very seriously back then, because nobody paid any attention to the witches and a lumberjack went ahead and cut me down. As I crashed to the ground, the witches went shrieking from the neighborhood to the western part of town where there were still large forests, and they found a new tree for their ceremonies. But before they left, they told the city to beware, because in less than a year they would exact their revenge.

BEWARE ELEVENTH MONTH!

The townsfolk went ahead and had their May Day celebrations and afterward, they burned my wood in a great Whitsuntide bonfire. And everyone, except me, forgot about the witches. Until eleven months later, that is, when the witches took their revenge. This came in the form of a tremendous tornado on March 27, 1890 - one of the deadliest tornadoes in American history today - which the witches brewed up in their new copse of trees. Then they sent it into town along Maple Street, as a reminder, and it flattened more than half of downtown. Almost a hundred people were killed as well, a number of them members of something known as the May Day Celebration Committee.

After it wreaked its havoc, the twister took a strange right-hand turn and roared along this street into what is now Old Louisville. As it passed by, a bolt of lightning shot out from the tornado and struck my stump, and I was transformed, magically springing up in my current twisted form.

With my burls and gnarled trunk, and the dead branches I rattle at night, I'm now the perfect haven for witches and others interested in the occult and magic and mystery. Many nights they come back to me and they brew their potions and cast their spells once again. Won't you come and join us?"

Many indigenous tribes and rural communities across the world believe that trees have spirits and are very angry if the tree is damaged or cut down. People perceive many trees as haunted, having resident spirits. I wonder how they come about that notion...

We know that humans have used certain trees for particular purposes, and these uses have given rise to knowledge of both the physical attributes and also spiritual help; behold the mighty oak, rest under the willow by the stream, be inspired by the great Sequoia, plant a line of pine trees to your country home. Native Americans put cedar in their sage bundles and the Hopi kachina dolls were only made from cottonwood root. The Zuni made prayer sticks from lightning struck Ponderosa pine. When I lived in New Mexico, I would marvel at harvest time for pinon nuts, as the natives went out in the country, off roads and highways, with their family and spread a blanket below the pinon tree. First Nations People call trees "The Standing People".

Do you have <u>that</u> favorite tree, the one that you <u>have</u> to visit when you're visiting someplace? When I visited the old Shaker village near Harrodsburg, Kentucky, I marveled at the old trees. There was a wise old cedar tree, tall and solitary, off to the east of the Centre Family Dwelling. Over the years, as I visited Shakertown and I became a volunteer Shaker singer, I would take opportunities to check in on "my" tree. I love the feeling of old cedar trees. As they mature, they morph from round bushy things to tall trees worthy of inspiration. Back in rural Missouri, close to where I grew up in St. Louis, I loved climbing the sturdy cedar branches. They offered protection and it just <u>felt good</u> to be under the cedar's canopy.

Tall Cedar Tree, Shakertown at Pleasant Hill, Kentucky photo by
Thomas Freese

Indeed, we can have a history certain types of trees,
memory associations stretching back to childhood. When I
see the bumpy green fruit of the Osage Orange tree I am
transported back from Kentucky to my grade school in
suburban St. Louis. On a fall Saturday afternoon my friends
and I lobbed the bumpy fruit down from a wooded hill.

While there are those who look with contempt at
tree huggers, we have seen environmental disasters rip

through communities that were surrounded by clear-cut logging. In July of 1939, a wall of water rushed into Morehead, Kentucky and the flooding in the eastern part of that state swept away homes and lives. If you know the feeling of protecting your children, your spouse and your pets...then you can understand the strong bond between a human and their beloved tree. The old Owensboro sassafras mentioned above was due to be bulldozed down in the 1950s. And the lady who owned the property came out with a shotgun...and that is why today it is still there, right off Frederica Street.

The Owensboro Ancient Sassafras Tree photo by Thomas Freese

Gather around the campfire, with light and warmth from burning wood, and listen to tales of wood spirits and tree nymphs. Down at the creek, gaze at a large sycamore tree and marvel at the whole ecosystem of animals and insects around just one tree. This book offers a rare look into the spiritual meanings of trees and woods. There are such guides for herbs, for crystals, but most compendiums for the meaning of trees are found on the Internet…and those lists don't provide a provenance of where <u>they</u> obtained the information. I enlisted the assistance of my psychic friends and they provided most of the meanings given in the following pages. Thus it is channeled material…just like the Bible.

Trees' Effect on our Language

Some sayings with their origin in trees or tree parts/properties:
Can't see the forest for the trees
Put your roots down
Out on a limb
The nut doesn't fall far from the tree
She is the apple of my eye
Cut a switch
Knock on wood
Out on the stump
The Bodhi Tree (of enlightenment)
Turn over a new leaf
Family tree
Idea takes root
Branching out
Bend with the wind

Proverbs:
From a fallen tree, all make kindling. Spanish proverb

"Arbol que crece torsido jamas su tronco se enderesa. A tree that grows crooked will never straighten its trunk."

"He who plants a tree plants a hope."
Lucy Larcom, *Plant a Tree*

"A fool sees not the same tree that a wise man sees."
William Blake, *Proverbs of Hell*, 1790

"Deep roots are not reached by the frost" J.R.R. Tolkien

All birds will flock to a fruitful tree. Senegalese proverb

Songs/lullaby:
Hush a bye Baby
On the Tree Top,
When the Wind blows
The Cradle will rock
When the Bough breaks
The Cradle will fall,
Down tumbles Baby,
Cradle and all

The Metaphysical Meanings of Trees and Woods

"Tree qualities, after long communion, come to reside in man. As stillness enhances sound, so through little things the joy of living expands. One is aware, lying under trees, of the roots and directions of one's whole being. Perceptions drift in from earth and sky. A vast healing begins."
From "Words of the Earth" by Cedric Wright

I am an author, storyteller and artist. I've worked with woods since the early 1980s and enjoyed making wood jewelry, ornaments and spoons. I made some wood "icicles" in the fall of 2011 to complement my offerings of seasonal ornaments. When I brought my wood crafts to a metaphysical event in September of 2012, in Anchorage, Alaska, a lady picked up one of the wooden icicles and then pointed it at her friend.

The other lady gave a knowing nod, and then the first lady turned to me and remarked, "I've never met a wand maker!"

I insisted that they were just wood ornaments but she replied, "No, I can <u>feel</u> the energy. You're making wands!"

I did have some narrow thin scraps of woods that were left from making spoons. And her comments got me thinking that perhaps some folks might be interested in handcrafted wands. So I tentatively made a few simple wands, from odd pieces of local apple wood, willow and

3

cherry. Customers were interested in the wands, often asking, "Are these magic wands?" I worked with more and more types of woods and experimented with different wands sizes and shapes—such as serpentine and spiral wands, pocket wands and wands wood burned with Celtic interlaces and runes.

I do love working with wood, and the care, love and good vibes I put into crafting each pin, bead, pair of earrings, spoon, pendant, standing figure, wand and more, programs good intentions and positive energy into each work of art. One animal communicator/intuitive picked up one of my wood jewelry pins, tuned into the feel of it, and said, "You put a lot of good prayers into your pieces." And so it is, as I sit on my back porch, sanding some wands or spoons for hours at a time. The wood brings its own energies and awareness and added to that is the artists loving touch.

A wand is not just a twig picked up from the ground (for most of the wands that I craft). A wand is made from the main part of the tree or worked from a significant size branch. The curvy and spiral wands I craft do not come that way in nature but are made from straight pieces of wood. It can take anywhere from about one hour to weeks to make a wand, depending on the amount of work. So far, I make simple wands—simple that is, in that I don't add wire or inlaid metal or stones. There is power in simplicity.

In the years that I have made and sold wands, people have very visceral reactions to the wands and to the varying tree energies from which they are crafted. I have to say, that many of the woods I use now are brought to me through so-called chance circumstance; that is, someone has cut down their hemlock or hickory tree, or I buy wood that comes from an old building, or I may be given odd and interesting pieces from a musical instrument maker.

The medium <u>is</u> the message, meaning the tree is a living being with awareness, experience and both universal and individualistic properties. Consider the holly wood that I've worked with for years. I found an online posting for giveaway holly logs from the front yard of an antebellum mansion just a few miles away from my home in Louisville, Kentucky. I called the number and the lady reported, "No it's all going to firewood. Someone is coming with a truck to take it away."

I told her I had a small car and wouldn't take but a few logs, and she replied, "If you come right over before he arrives, then you can take some." I drove over right away and got about a half dozen small logs. There had been a pair of holly trees in front of that old home, which had stood there I guessed since the 1800s. When I looked at the stumps, I figured it would have probably taken two or three sets of arms to reach around the circumference of each old holly tree. I don't have a chainsaw, a truck, or much woodworking equipment. But I have made so many wonderful pieces from that holly and I still have more pieces to work with.

Old Tree showing character from many years, photo by
Thomas Freese

And as I made holly wands, spoons and jewelry, I imagined all the many years and seasons that tree had experienced. Birds made nests and squirrels ran across its branches, it had watched the comings and goings of many human generations, been through terrible storms, oppressive winters, and brutal heat.

The ancients, of course, used trees and woods in so many ways and respected not only the utilitarian offerings of the various trees but also communicated and collected folk wisdom about what each type of tree could contribute to their physical, emotional and spiritual well-being. Where would we be without trees to give us oxygen, hold the soil and provide wood for thousands of uses? Children and adults instinctively go to sit under a tree, to rebalance after emotional upsets. Like the power of companion animals, our dogs, and cats, to help ground our troubled dispositions, to heal us, to remind us of the simple power of nature and of love—trees also are our helpers. The Native Americans call trees the "standing people".

Trees are solar collectors and, even in what we call their death, they then release overtime the energies stored up from their 100 years of life, or their 3,000-year-old existence.

Beth Moon photographed trees around the world and notes intriguing research that documents how trees respond to the moon, stars, and planets:

"Researchers from the University of Edinburgh have shown that trees grow faster when high levels of cosmic radiation reach the earth's surface, concluding that cosmic radiation impacts tree growth even more than annual temperature or rainfall. Secondly, renowned researcher, Lawrence Edwards, found that tree buds changed shape and size rhythmically, in regular cycles all through winter, directly correlating to the moon and planets. The oak, for example, appears to change with Mars, the Beech with Saturn and the Birch with Venus. Curiously, Edwards also found that overhead power lines disrupted this planetary influence."

Trees are the ultimate metaphor for our own life journey as we refer to our roots, the tree of life, being tough on the outside like bark, branches of government, and more—stems, hedge, leaflets. Woods keep us companion all our life from cradle to coffin. Trees gave us material for boats to explore the world, wood for musical instruments and boards to walk on each day in our home. But how often do we tune into the energy of the tree, whether outside or when holding a wood bowl, chopsticks or hairpin?

As with any other intuitive exercise, it merely takes a quiet session, relaxing the chatting mind, to discover what that still small voice of intuition, or Spirit guidance, wants to tell us about the wood or tree. Hold a wood spoon, and it can communicate psychometric information about the original tree, and any person or environment it experienced along the way. And it is true that a different human receiver may get different messages or uses from a particular wood wand.

I know some woods, particularly the ones with a strong scent like cedar or true olive wood, can transport my mind to another place on the planet, to another lifetime or connect with some ancient mystery. With other woods, that don't have a strong scent, I may not have a connection or strong feeling until I hold the wood.

So then what is a wand, how should I use it, and what are the metaphysical meanings of the different woods?

Whether your wand was given to you, or you purchased it, or you've made it, you can then start to develop a relationship with the wand. It is a tool, similar to a pair of scissors or a hammer. But it is also much more, as you can send energy to help protect yourself or to heal another person. My first suggestion is to "use your superpowers for good." That is, use your wand for appropriate protection, for positive and good reasons and outcomes. I make wands for, and sell to, both children and grownups.

The wand is an extension of our own energy and intent, combined with the attributes of the tree and nature, and added to that is the channeling of universal powers.

Wands are made from metal, bone, antler, stone, wood, glass…and other materials. Wands can be natural or embellished, folksy or cute.

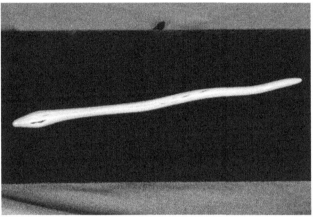

Glass wand by artist Sergio Vettori, in author Freese's private collection. 10 ½ inches long by ¼ to 3/8 inches diameter. Picture courtesy of Angela Hurd Greer.

Size does not matter but rather feel the force, if you will, to discern whether this wand is right for you. And next determine if this wand is to be used by you, exactly how best to use it. When I offer my wands for sale at public events, I'm often asked, "What do you use a wand for?" I'm reluctant to detail the many kinds of uses for wands, as I'd actually prefer they find their own unique use. But I can say that overall, wands are used in healing work, as with Reiki, to energize objects, or to scribe sacred symbols "in the air" and also to focus our intent—sending prayers to distant locations…and more! I think and feel, that the best way to learn the specifics of wand use is in person, from a teacher.

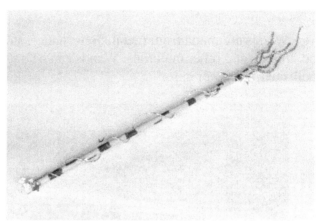

Fun Folk Art wand created by Thomas Freese, 21 inches in length. Picture courtesy of Angela Hurd Greer.

The shape of the wand can bring different energies. For example, a serpentine wand provides what Native Americans call "snake medicine". Spiral carved wands provide an amplified energy. In the old days, we called it "magic" and these days we call it "energy", but the attempt to label what is often invisible and yet moves to us, through us and into our world is a changing construct. Mini wands or pocket wands can be very portable and I hope to hear sometime if anyone has cleared road traffic or manifested a parking spot!

You might be wise, as a first-time wand user, to hold off on trying to levitate objects or make your younger sister disappear. The outcome is likely some frustration and then you'd probably set the wand aside as an ordinary piece of wood. Take a roundabout approach and try some gentle uses for your wand for a while. Some folks put the wand under their pillow at night; carry it around, get to know its feel and when the time is right, you will recognize which occasion to activate your wand. You can anoint your wand with special oils and have a simple ceremony to state your intention for how you'd like to use the wand.

Set your wand down on a white cloth, relax and see if you can perceive the aura, the glowing light that surrounds your wand. Did you know that a number of woods have fluorescent properties? Over 75 wood species exhibit varying patterns and colors when an ultraviolet light, or black light, is shined on them, in colors such as blue, yellow, green or orange.

For example, sit quietly and hold your wand. You might say, "I am grateful for this cedar wand and I open my mind and heart to know the wisdom of how to use this wand, and I ask the spirit of the cedar tree to help me in learning the best use of this wand for positive assistance and for good for myself and others." Let your intuition then guide you when and how to use your wand. Here below are some testimonials for the helpful power of trees and wood wands and other handcrafted wood pieces. Remember that what is significant is not only the wood, what kind of tree, but also how you develop a relationship with that wand. And also wood pieces that are not wands are also very important for spiritual protection; for example, a wooden cross or a pendant with a protective symbol carved or wood burned.

Three pendants with protective power symbols, hand-crafted by Thomas Freese. Left to right: wood burned olive wood Celtic interlace pendant (1 5/8 x 2 inches), wood burned holly "Flower of Life" pendant (3 inches in diameter), and wood burned oval holly Celtic interlace pendant (2 3/8 x 3 ¼ inches). Picture courtesy of Angela Hurd Greer. In the Celtic interlaces note the repetition of "X" formations as lines cross. Crossing one's hands, feet, fingers or forming an "X" in art has long been seen to be providing defensive energies for protection.

"…every human has a personal tree…" Verena Stael von Holstein, channeling Zuleika, the pomegranate tree being, from Nature Spirits of the Trees

Testimonials to the Powers of Woods

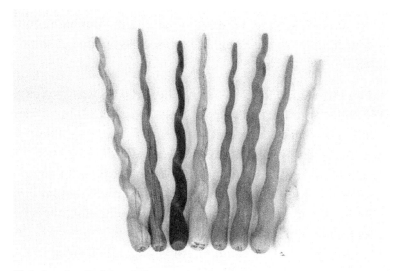

Eight handcrafted (partially completed) spiral wands by artist/author Thomas Freese. From left to right: Olive wood, Black Limba, Wenge, Pear, Chakte Viga, Birch, Osage Orange and Holly woods. Lengths range from 12 to 13 inches. Picture courtesy of Angela Hurd Greer.

Testimonials:
This morning I was holding each wand, and I could feel a different energy in each one. The holly was hot in my hand, the black walnut energy was cool, the willow was gently flowing and the ash was what I would describe as even-tempered. Diana, Dallas

Diana had another story about her wands from several years later…

I did Reiki at the Fort Worth Holistic Fair. I used my wands to conduct energy, and people can feel the energy from the wand. I had them set out on a small table in front of my massage table. So many people stopped to admire them and asked me about them, including several children. People wanted to buy them, but I told them they are my tools and not for sale. However I gave them your name and phone number as the Wand Maker, so I hope you get some calls.

Also, I wanted to tell you that a little girl who was six years old came up to me and asked if the wands were Harry Potter wands. I told her that as matter of a fact, yes, these wands are very much like Harry Potter wands. I told her, "This one is holly…" and I explained that it wasn't magic as in making something appear, but it had energy and it conducted energy. I talked a little about energy that would make sense to a six-year-old. Then I offered it to her to hold and asked if she could feel anything. She handed it back to me and said "No". Then she added, "It stings". I explained to her that what she felt was energy! Diana Vincenti

My uses for wands vary—some are for show, some for focus with energy work, and the one I bought from Thomas Freese I use as an energy amplifier. It doubles the energy of anything I use it on, and being apple wood I believe it helped me see my first vision when I used it on my crystal ball. I definitely believe anyone buying a wand from Thomas is making a great decision!
Adrienne, Cincinnati

I got the holly wood wand today. Wow! I've put it on some clear crystal to "come home" here and later I'll smudge it. I didn't want to let go of it for even that long, though. And once the grass dries from our days of rain I'll put it outside on the ground, too. Thank you!
Kim, Washington

It fits nicely in my hand. It will serve its purpose similar to worry beads. When I'm writing and stuck, I will hold it and draw energy. Not a traditional use, but it suits my purpose. I was supposed to have it!
Jane, Tennessee

The Leopard Wood really is apparently a "generator". After I made a necklace of the Leopard Wood Celtic heart pendant, the right side of my skull and my right arm kept buzzing. I was told via my angels that it was because the Leopard Wood tree spirit was helping me release energies I was unaware of (as I believe the right side of the body "gives" energy, while the right side "receives" it). Basically, it appears to me that this leopard wood helps us to release the energies of who and what we actually are, so we can go out to assist others.   SW, Louisville

My sweet purpleheart wand is wonderful...ready and willing to use with my healing Reiki sessions. I felt that as soon as I touched it!
Martha, Louisville

The energy in the hemlock wand is very nice. I love holding it! Jason Hundley

I love my beautiful wand. It has such great craftsmanship. I love the feel of the spirals and smoothness of the wood. I will have to learn its name. Thank you. Anonymous, Louisville

I use the plum wood wand to set intention and raise energy over a pile of paperwork. I also use it to set intention and raise energy over my phone for a call I need to make. I will tell you more as I use it often but I do like it. Thank you!
Diane, Kentucky

15

It's interesting that I saw the curvy wand on Saturday at Victory of Light. I was drawn to it, without knowing it was a made from the Sequoia tree…I let it go. When I saw you speak on Sunday and you said it was Sequoia I wanted it. Sequoia is a spirit totem for me. I was sitting back in the audience. At the end of your lecture, there were two people deep around you and your wands. I saw that someone was holding it. I told my friend, "Oh I'll never get to the Sequoia wand, I'm too far back." At that moment the lady who had been holding that wand put it down. A woman in front of me picked it up and handed it to me!! I'm a massage therapist. I plan on using the Sequoia wand for healing work. Thank you for honoring the trees. You do beautiful work. Marilyn, Kentucky

I want to tell you that I have been using the mahogany wand lately. This winter I put a shield around my son before goes sledding. I also passed it over the wood I'm using to build my tank for marbling fabric. It is a very handy clarifying and protecting tool! Lesley, Nashville

I am SO happy with the beautiful wands I now have that Thomas made! I bought a wood burned holly wand and a lightning struck sequoia wand. They both have such intense energy. Marcy, Crestwood, Kentucky

I love my Makore wand! David, Lexington, Kentucky

When I was dedicating my small Osage orange wood (hedge apple) wand I got from you, it decided for itself that it would be used for animal healing. And I used it this past weekend. Perfect! Thank you, Thomas! Patsy, Ohio

I purchased your spiral plum wand. It called to me with its healing and negativity dispersing abilities. I am very happy with my purchase and have already used it in cleansing my

home, it made a magnificent difference! Thank you again,
Kevin, Ohio

I have been using the pink ivory wand to clear my own
energy field of stuff and it's working well, I feel it up, pick
it out and throw them into the ground. I have been also
using it to shift energies in a room and will continue to test
them out. I love my wand! Thank you for making such a
beauty! Jaime Shine, Hot Springs, Arkansas

I had been looking for a more suitable job for over three
years, since 2012. Besides extremely active networking, I
dedicated most of my free time to internet job searches and
sending out job applications. By mid of 2015, I was really
discouraged and disappointed. Nothing had worked out, in
spite of my qualifications, my huge efforts, and time
investment. I was considering moving back to Germany
and had started to apply for positions there when I attended
an evening at the Esoteric Society in Louisville. Thomas
Freese spoke about his passion in regards to working with
different woods and explained different kinds of trees and
their energy.

Looking at and touching some of the items he made from
different woods, it turned out that I particularly liked a few
pieces, and they were all made out of the same piece of
lightning struck Sequoia wood. I also liked a pendant very
much, that he wore around his neck. It had the shape of a
Thunderbird. And that piece was also made out of the
Sequoia tree. I decided to purchase these four pieces made
from the Sequoia wood (two wands, one cooking spoon,
and the pendant).

I started to wear the pendant almost every day, I liked it so
much! I felt it made me somehow stronger. About one
week after I had purchased it, I went for lunch with a

17

business acquaintance who I had known for years. He was the buyer for a company by the name of PHOENIX Process Equipment. I was their account manager for quite a few years. He noticed the pendant and said, "It looks just like a Phoenix, very similar to our company Logo".

I opened up to him and told him that I had very actively been looking for a different job opportunity because I felt miserable at my present employment. He encouraged me to send him my resume and told me how highly he thought of me. He ensured me that he would ask around amongst his business contacts and he would highly recommend me. A few months later he texted me and asked me if I would like to interview for an inside sales position within his parts department at Phoenix.

I interviewed, I went through the application process online as well, and after one week I received a job offer—which I accepted. I started the new position on November 9th, 2015 and have been very happy ever since. Somehow I believe your Phoenix Pendant had something to do with this wonderful change in my life. Thanks so much again for everything,
Renate Klein, Louisville, Kentucky

My willow wand is out back soaking up the full Hunters supermoon at this very moment. I also felt the impulse to 'throw my voice' into it today. I hummed a very powerful tone (the same one I use when I am sick) into the base of it today for several minutes. Sarah, Lexington, KY

I bought a spiral zebrawood wand from you. Thanks for sending information on zebrawood. I will treasure it!
Laura, Kentucky

I could feel balance just holding the Bocote wand. I love the sassy attitude part. That's me. Mary Ann, Louisville, KY

I think I'll be wearing that holly moon pendant a lot. I think I choose the types of wood that would be of great benefit to me. They are both beautiful. I can't wait to use my spoon. Is there a type of wood that is good for creativity? You do such beautiful unique work. The tree lives on in your pieces of art. Debbie Mitchell, Taylorsville, KY

Thomas thanks so much for the wand. It's really beautiful. I like the grain in the dark wood, and it's nice the way it's split between light and dark. Best part is it's made from my own apricot tree—very cool. Dan Vandolah, Santa Fe, New Mexico

It was great to play with the beautiful spiral wands I just purchased. The Yellow Heart is for "seeing". The tip projects a crystal sphere with many small triangular facets. There are shimmering rainbows near the edges of the facets. Looking into this sphere somehow promotes clarity and shows interconnections. The Purple Heart is for healing. There is a blue flame that radiates from its tip. It creates heat. It magnifies Reiki. It transmits pulses of energy from my hand into the wand. Thank you for the lovely craftsmanship and healing energy that you put into these beautiful works of art.
Christine, Louisville, KY

Cast away Taxus shrub (yew) wood crafted into Celtic interlace
Bead and photo by Thomas Freese

Thank you, Thomas, for the beautiful yew wood bead.
When I held it for the first time I immediately felt wave
upon wave of calming grounding energy. Your work is
amazing and the wood knows that you know it. Thank you,
I love it. Marilyn Burke, Georgetown, KY

The energy from the Ebony is amazing. When I picked it
up it sent me on a vision quest. The first thing it showed me
was the symbol of a pentagram. It then proceeded to show
me Celtic and sacred geometry. It is definitely a piece that
can be used for positive or negative. It will amplify
whatever your mood is. When I held in my hand I could
feel the energy running down my body and out through it.
Of all the pieces that I have channeled or worked with for
Thomas this was by far the most magical. Angie Clark, Florida

I immediately felt a calm presence with this wand. I handled several pieces of Pink Ivory wood and while they all had a feminine energy, they clearly had different purposes and spirits attached to them. The wand I brought home I named, Gloria. Well, I didn't name her. That was simply the name she revealed to me. Gloria formed a fast and strong connection with me as a protective energy. I feel that all Pink Ivory probably bonds quickly and is very protective and a, 'one person' piece of wood. She is not to be used while working with others, but rather is a personal ally in my own healing and spiritual work. Gloria told me that she is the 'eye of the storm'. The spirit of this wood and this spirit connected to this wand instill peace in the midst of chaos. She stands before me to deflect harsh energies and when I wear her in my hair to twist and tie it back, she stands behind me guarding and protecting and in that way can be with me wherever I go.

She has an ethereal appearance, willowy with billowing robes, but a strength that isn't to be underestimated. I handled several Pink Ivory wands and pieces. I found that the other wand while still having that fiercely protective energy for the person it is destined to partner with was not the calm in the storm, but rather what I would call, 'Red Sonja' who was a Viking warrior woman. That wand's purpose was to bring energy and the ability to, 'fight the good fight' and find one's voice. A third piece of Pink Ivory presented herself as a personal muse for the writer or academician. An interesting story about Gloria...I left her on my table at a festival I was working to walk across the room to deposit an empty water bottle in a receptacle. She clearly stated that she wanted to go with me. I hesitated and said, I'm just going across the room and was a little confused by the insistence. On the way back, I ran into a person I respect as a master Reiki and energy worker. He offered to show me a new technique for quickly clearing

myself and drawing down energy. I then realized that Gloria knew what was coming and wanted to be part of the energy exchange. As the Reiki Master was working on me in that impromptu session, I created a direct line of energy to Gloria on my table so that we could be linking and share in that experience. I realized that once she was aligned with that same energy, when I need a boost or reminder to perform that exercise on myself, she will be power ally in that work. I will never again doubt her wisdom.
Holly McCullough, Kentucky

We find woods, and also woods find us...

As I work with each new type of wood, I'm so happy to feel the energy of each tree, and to see later who is drawn to that particular vibration. I often receive wood from folks who have cut down a beloved tree in their own yard. The sequoia mentioned above that I have worked with is actually a dawn redwood. I take walks in my extended neighborhood, and I often admired a tall tree in a yard about a half mile away. I once spoke with the owner who told me he had no idea it would grow so tall and that it was a dawn redwood. I was a bit shy to directly ask for some trim off branches, but I made friends with his neighbor two doors down. I asked her to save me some branches if he ever had some cut off from that tree.

Several years ago, I returned from my son's wedding in North Carolina and I found some small branches stacked on the top of my driveway. There was a note from that same neighbor lady, who wrote, "The tree was struck by lightning yesterday and nearly all the wood went for firewood. I saved you a few pieces. Would you please make a cross for the gentleman who owns the tree?" Always grateful for any gifts of usable and unique woods, I made him a cross and a nice spoon for her. What I

22

discovered though, through online research, is that many traditional cultures value wood items made from a lightning struck tree. I read that the Zuni Native Americans make prayer sticks from a lightning struck ponderosa pine. I lived 12 years in Santa Fe, New Mexico, where they have amazing woods out in the high desert and in the mountains—such as pinon, aspen and ancient cottonwoods in the river valleys. I was informed that the Hopi traditionally make kachina spirit dolls from cottonwood root.

I discovered a number of online sources for the meanings of the different woods. These websites do not tell how or from where they acquired this information. Who was first to post the lists and from what book was the information originally gleaned? Was the information from old folk wisdom, or was it channeled in some way? Since I had worked with dozens of different woods over the decades, I decided to send outnumbered samples to some fellow psychics and see what information they could discover about each of the woods. I sent out over 70 pieces that were not identified by name, only having a number assigned to each sample. In addition, these intuitive readers were not familiar with cut woods and they had done no research on their own to read about the online meaning of woods.

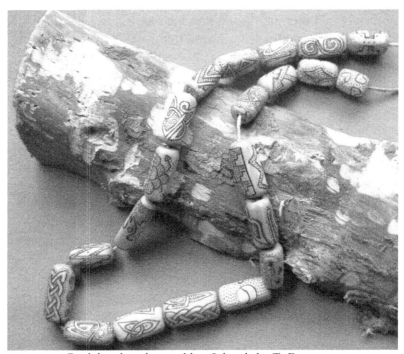

Reclaimed apple wood log & beads by T. Freese
Guide to the Meanings of Woods

Guide to the Meanings of Woods

Here below are the meanings for 123 trees/woods as given by three psychic sources, and two online sources. I have assigned a two letter abbreviation for each wood (which follows the name of the wood). In some cases, you'll see that the meanings, although channeled by psychics in totally different U.S. states, are very similar. With other woods, they are not at all the same but rather part of an aggregate of complementary information where the user can choose which meaning is valid for their purposes. Also please note that this list is NOT comprehensive but rather are the woods that I have encountered along the way and the ones I use currently to make wands and other artistic objects. Some woods below that I didn't have samples for are given information from another source, with permission, and that source does not have a two letter abbreviation (of a psychic) with each entry. Here are the three psychics who assisted—their names and abbreviations, (and additional information about them later in the book).

LB Laura Berlin
AC Angie Clark
DE Dale Epley

Properties of Wood Wands

Acacia Koa (AK)

It has both a masculine and a feminine side, almost completely separate. Masculine properties: The energies associated with the masculine aspects of this wood are duality and balance, like the tides. This energy is deeply connected with the ocean, which is alternately giving and destructive. To truly utilize the masculine properties of this wood, one must be able to recognize and become comfortable with the ebb and flow of its energy. Feminine properties: Centered on the element of fire, Koa in its feminine aspect brings creativity, beauty, and wisdom, and strength. It also brings a fiery energy, capable of destructive power or the power to overcome strife.

African Blackwood (AB)

LB: this wood can help you to accomplish anything—success, money, relationships, business and wealth.

DE: With African Blackwood, I feel the energy going to the heart and upper chakras. When I hold it to heart chakra, that chakra opens more—and same with throat chakra. Hold this wood up to your third eye chakra and there will be rays of blue. Holding over the crown chakra, it sends energy pouring into the body down to the heart chakra. In terms of the lower chakras, it provides some energy, but not like the upper chakras.

AC: I pick the energy up in the shoulders. This wood helps you to let go of burdens and of being overwhelmed. It also helps you to find your inner strength and can help heal bone tissue. African Blackwood says, "You are always stronger than you believe yourself to be. But it is not necessary to carry the entirety of the world's problems on your own shoulders. See the lesson and what you will accept as your truth in each experience. Release the rest with love and the intention of resurrection. This tree means to transmute energy that is heavy and dense to lighter more productive forms. Strength is as much mental as it is physical…all of which takes training to reach the rewards they bring."

Alder (AD)
Alder is said to be good for controlling and banishing elementals, especially of fire or water as the tree has strong links with both elements, and it can apparently be used for the healing of wounds. It is allegedly attracted to water, so is used for dowsing. Legend has it that the Alder tree is a favorite of the Elven King's daughter. It is strongly associated with resurrection.

Alligator Juniper (AJ)
This draws off the element of fire. This wood seeks a gifted healer, as it is a medicinal wood said to be used to cure such illnesses as the black plague. More uses include binding spells, white magic, and protection. It is excellent for healing magic.

Apple (AP)
LB says some see this tree as weak but it helps to camouflage those who do not wish to be seen. It's a good tree to have around with many uses and this tree has visitors from other dimensions.
DE: Apple gives powerful, instant energy. It is an instant magnetic feeling and very active around and in physical eyes and sinuses. It can assist those with allergy issues.
AC: This wood provides energetic and physical healing of the heart. I see lots of pink energy. Apple creates a greater sense of heart-centered thought and behaviors. This tree says, "Living from the heart is the greatest achievement of the human form. It does not come without its challenges,

and the kingdom of trees honors your choice to do so. I can assist you in enhancing this connection to love, the language of the universe."

It is a fine sight, the apple tree with ripe fruit. Photo by Thomas Freese

Apricot (AR)

LB: takes away stress and dispels fear. It helps to repel jealous and envious people. Apricot assists in our efforts to be creative and keeps us moving along with the flow of life. It says, "take your time and don't rush into decisions without research—ask questions!"

AC: Apricot touches upon the sacral chakra, which represents root issues of reproduction and replenishment. It symbolizes solid energetic grounding and rooting our connection with physical reality. Apricot says, "I enter the human energy field to multiply all things of joy and sustainment. I can assist with the fertility of goals and aspirations even to the basic fabric of physical fertility and birth."

Ash (AS)
LB: the ash tree gives us its energy as a pillar of strength, reminding us that we CAN stand alone or also stand tall with our community. It teaches us to return home to a place of love and understanding.

DE: Ash loves sunshine and it keeps the heart chakra open. It has a soothing energy, great for meditating.

AC: Ash gives us clarity and purity of thought, by cleansing out any clutter of thoughts and by narrowing to specific points. It helps us to disconnect from ego and connect to universal truth. The emphasis here is on the crown chakra connection and the ability to rearrange polarity. Ash can assist those who are dealing with bipolar issues by helping with focus. The ash tree says, "In the physical form and in a place filled with duality the path to following truth and higher forms of light can get complicated. I can help by turning off the voice of the ego to connect you with your guides and universal information from them and from Divine Source. I wish for you to see past the clutter and clouded reality of the human condition."

Australian Blackwood (AW)
This wood draws off the elements of earth, water and wind. It represents strength and determination. This is a neutral wood, indifferent to white or black Magic. It possesses both healing and destructive powers.

Avodire (AV)
Avodire is born from the element of water and thrives on the energy of the sun. It is a powerful male wood who seeks a creative companion with a vivid imagination. Used for defense and protection.

Basswood (BS)
LB: this wood encourages us to keep trying despite what others may say.

DE: Basswood branches sing in the wind, while sunlight glistens on its leaves. Breathe in a scent of its wood to clear sinuses.

AC: Basswood highlights truth and secrets. It connects to our throat chakra. I see lots of gold light with this one. Basswood says, "I assist you in finding your truth so that you no longer lie to yourself or cover the reality of the situation. I help you to accept what is and delete the need to make something what it is not for reasons of coping and the inability to see or accept a situation as it is. I also assist you to keep negativity out of your internal energetics and help keep it at a distance so that you may evaluate and not connect on a reactionary or destructive level. See situations as they are. Know your truth, and react accordingly."

Bay (BY)
Bay is used for purification and healing and is said to bring strength and protection. It can also be used to increase psychic powers.

Beech (BE)
LB: this wood is an igniter, motivated and determined, helps us to never give up. It assists in seeing through people and feeling their auras.

DE: Beech has a strong energy that one can feel in all chakras, but mostly in throat chakra. In addition, it is helpful for the eyes and temples. Beech wood loves to travel with you, feels free and loves the energy of lots of people. Meditate with beech as this one will talk to you! AC: Beech wood provides softness and flexibility, with a focus on the sacral chakra. It says, "All humans are softer than the rigid structure you see on the outside. Inside there is much room and ability to be molded and shaped into what you choose to become. I ask you to look deep within and move gracefully into that form. Sometimes a slight bit is shaved or not formed as perfectly as you requested initially. This requires more work and perhaps some flexibility in structure to adapt to a new vision or goal. This may also entail a new path to get there. Be moldable and flexible in shape. You will feel less stress fractures and be less likely to break."

Beech in Indiana, reaching upward towards the sun, photo by Thomas Freese

Birch (BI)

LB: this wood forewarns of earth changes, helps us to know when something is going to happen. It can aid us in dealing with tragedy and help find missing people.

DE: Birch acts like a worry stone, and has a beautiful smooth feel. It is calming and helps us relax. It is great to hold while meditating.

AC: Birch highlights touch and expansion of healing energies with the hands, particularly at the palm center chakra or meridian. Birch says, "With each touch you connect to energy and have the ability to alter the energy you encounter. I help the healers to move and rearrange energy for the health of the receiver. I expand the energy centers in the palms of the hands to allow a full exchange of energy and discernment for what is received."

Blackberry Bramble (BR)

Or Briar, as it is also known, provides strong protection of the home. It is useful for spells concerning money or prosperity, and it is said to aid in the healing of burns.

Black Laurel (BA)

Is a powerful wood which draws off the element of fire and Saturn's energy. It is known for the contributing properties of courage, passion, and strength. Use this wood for the absorption and destruction of negative energy. It excels in the reversal of negative spells, and it excellent for repelling dark magic.

Black Limba (BM)

LB: it is an old soul and gives us comfort, particularly for those who suffer from loneliness, sadness and depression. It provides hope, giving us strength from Mother Earth. Black Limba helps us to stay strong and grounded, sending our roots deep down.

DE: Black Limba has a happy vibration and is an important healer. It will cleanse you and your home of negative energy, but is more potent as a larger piece of wood. I first felt its energy in my lower back and then it spread to rest of my body. Black Limba comes from the area of close trees and bushes and loves being with all the different woods. It likes being passed around and studied.

AC: Black Limba is good for expanding of the crown chakra and for opening to psychic gifts and to new information or ideas. It expands comprehension of complex ideas and helps discharge toxins in the body especially from the pineal gland. Black Limba additionally helps with psychic protection and prevents empathic people from being overloaded. Black Limba says, "Your connection to source energy is as valuable to your existence—much as breathing air—and especially for those of empathic nature and natural psychic gifts. I assist in expansion and balance with universal connection and mystical energy and abilities. It is my honor to bring energies that assist the path to direct enlightenment. Utilize these gifts and allow them to enhance your life."

Black Locust (BL)

LB: it is sly, quick thinking on one's feet. It brings out our artistic side and helps us to receive signs and signals that point us to the right path. It helps with clairvoyant and precognitive abilities for messages from the angels, ascended masters and spirit guides.

DE: Black Locust can help you astral travel as well as going back in time. It is a key to the Akashic Records. It will help you release bad memories and will provide a cleansing.

AC: Black locust assists with boundaries and psychic protection. It helps in healing childhood trauma, or helping others through a serious event of health issues or traumatic life events. Black locust enhances strength and perseverance. This wood facilitates connection to spirit to allow others to lean upon you and draw energy of support without allowing you to become depleted and your energy resources to be empty. This prevents you from becoming ill or out of balance as well. Black locust says, "Care for yourself as you fulfill the needs of others. If you are empty you are no longer effective in the tasks and support you wish to offer. You must see yourself as valuable as those you wish to assist. If you do not, you pay a dear price and cannot be who or what you desire to be. This is a tough lesson for those of empathic nature and I offer assistance in building energetic boundaries and clearing. I also help you to release toxic relationships."

Black Poisonwood (BP)
It draws from the element of earth. It is a powerful combination of strength and versatility. It seeks a companion of strength and determination, however indifferent to its owner's will. Black Poisonwood is excellent for defensive spells or protective magic.

Blackthorn (BK)
Blackthorn provides very strong protection, especially of the home, and can be used in magic to deter unwanted visitors. It is said to protect against malevolent magic. It can also be used in exorcism.

Bloodwood (BO)
LB: this wood helps us to open up our heart, mind, body and soul to all possibilities; the answer is always yes I can! DE: With Bloodwood I felt an expansion of energy from the upper heart and out around shoulders. It is a quiet healer and helps one to release deep anxieties. One might begin to feel that anxiety after holding it a bit, but it is a good thing, as it is helping you to release.

AC: I get overall feelings of peace. This wood aids in realigning fractured heart energy. It can help heal blood cells that are not functioning correctly. Bloodwood says, "The human species overlooks the importance of being whole in their most valuable place--their heart. I wish to see them live in the heart center as they were initially designed. I bring the frequencies to assist them in returning here, in order to see the world with eyes of love." It can transfer this energy into food if used in serving pieces or even placed in a kitchen.

Bocote (BC)
LB: is good for enhancing psychic ability, and promotes our inner strength. It helps to open the third eye and is good for astral travel. Bocote says, "I'm special—glamorous! I have a sassy attitude and I'm independent—I can do whatever I want!"
AC: Bocote affects the crown and feet chakras. It aligns the energy of those chakras with the heavens and earth. Bocote provides basic energetic connection and balance. It is also good for energy healers to maintain their connections and replenishment of energy. It calms anxiety and releases stress. Bocote says, "To achieve you must align. When you move through life you have choices to remain connected to energies of help and restoration as well as support, or you choose to walk the path alone. I bring the ability to remain balanced and pull energy from those places of balance and wisdom you seek."

Boxwood (BX)
LB: this wood gives healing and absorbs energies from people in order to heal. It helps change from negative to positive, bringing out our inner strength for those who feel weak.
DE: Boxwood has to get to know you, so you should hold it for a while. The energy goes directly to where there is

pain or discomfort and helps it to melt away. If you are clairaudient, it will gradually talk and give information about health issues.

AC: Boxwood contributes silence and connection. Boxwood says, "I wish for humans to find their silence and connection with us as well as source energy. As you walk through the forests or utilize my energy I assist in unlocking the door to peace and quiet. All that is necessary is to be."

Boxwood hummingbird and carved star, art and photo by Thomas Freese

Bubinga (BB)

LB: it has a giggling, light energy—happy to be alive. The energy provides clarity and a sense of peace. It is from the angelic realm and takes the weight off one's shoulders."

DE: I felt Bubinga work with my third eye chakra. I saw a golden pinpoint of light then as it came closer it grew larger till it disappeared and I felt it inside me. I saw an energetic vise break away from around my head, then what looked like a half suit of armor broke away from the right side of my body and slowly disappeared. I've recently had discomfort in the right side of my upper body, my hand, arm and shoulder. This one removes ancient barriers and heals the wounds from those barriers.

AC: Bubinga emphasizes creativity and self-expression and connects to the sacral chakra. This sample has the ability to inspire ideas, projects, and motivation. This wood can also help create vision and physically assist the eyes as well as the intestinal sacral area. Bubinga says, "To create a life that is fulfilling and assist the soul to be satisfied, it is helpful to be inspired and create projects and ideas that lead to life goals and feelings of accomplishment. To connect with your higher self you must unlock the doors to see what is inside. Tapping into creation energy can help you accomplish this. I bring vibrations specific to this process and am honored to assist."

Buckeye (BU)

Is a wood of medicine, healing, and meditation, and also used for luck. It seeks a companion healer/witch doctor. It is excellent for banishing spells. Buckeye has traditionally been carried as a charm to bring luck or create success by naturally gathering together the right energies that can create positive circumstances.

Butternut (BN)

LB: this has fairy energy and is good for those who would like to be assisted from shyness to confidence.

DE: With Butternut, I can feel gentle energy move through my whole body. I then see a soft glow around me as a part of my aura. This one helps release pent up energy; it provides a clearing away. For instance, I had just finished a walking exercise and I could feel the release of tightness in my lower legs. Butternut, if held against a sore spot on the physical body, helps to release the soreness and the cause for it. This process takes a while and needs to be repeated often.

AC: Butternut represents the interplay between intensity and indifference. The energy of this tree can help bring both extremes back to a place of balance. Thus it works to either calm or enhance these energies. This can help a fanatic to find a sense of balance and reason, and give those who can't seem to care a sense of connection and greater passion for life. This process is of course magnified in a wand crafted of this wood. Butternut says, "There is an energetic fine line between the town prophet and the village idiot. You may have the best intentions and the biggest heart and still overpower others energetically and emotionally. Be passionate but remain reasonable in this quest. On the other hand, it is unhealthy to have no interest and no connection to ideas that improve a person on an individual level all the way to large scale concepts that elevate the entire human collective. The ultimate goal is balance. Be passionate with an ear and ability to listen and adapt beliefs other than those you know presently, and be able to connect with these energies without allowing them to overpower you and overwhelm your emotions…extremes that are sometimes seen of interrupting the energy of the body to make it unstable. I assist in this specific balance of vibrations."

Camellia (CA)
Camellia is useful in matters concerning riches.

Canary wood (CW)
AC: Canary wood helps heal fascia tissues and it is very much a physical healer. It works to dissipate inflammation and promotes healthy cell growth. It can also help raise

DNA codes if used with intention. "The physical body works much as the rings of growth from the trees point of view, however, it works more in terms of energy. The layers can be rearranged to align in light and health and allow you to grow in a much more beneficial pattern. I assist in the realignment of energy which restructures the physical codes in the body."

Uprising Cedar Tree photo by Thomas Freese

Cedar (CE)
LB: this wood helps us to find peace and quiet. It brings fun-filled and carefree days, helping us to enjoy life to the fullest and laugh with joy.
DE: While holding a piece of cedar, I repeatedly saw a Native American chief, with headdress, smoking a long pipe. He turned and put out his arm and hand toward me,

palm facing me. I could feel the energy in my upper chest and throat area. I heard the word 'visionary'.

AC: Cedar represents perseverance and determination. One can feel its energy above the Sacral Chakra in the "gut" as it brings the energy to help rally, and find your way through the storm. Cedar says, "It is easier often to give up a dream or fall to a place of falter or despair. These emotions are powerful and all-consuming at times for any in life. I bring you the energy vibrations to see it through to the end or find that part of you that can overcome all obstacles."

Chakte Viga (CV)

LB: has a strong, hard core of energy—it won't back down. This tree stands up to resistance and represents being a leader and NOT a follower. It also reminds us that there is strength and comfort in numbers—family is very important.

AC: zooms in on the root chakra, moving and letting go of vibrations of fear and flight (our desire to run away from difficulties). It can help with kidneys and adrenal issues. Chakte Viga says, "When one hold the vibrations of fear it is easy to avoid and run from the things that you fear. I assist you to stand and face the fear with peace and courage."

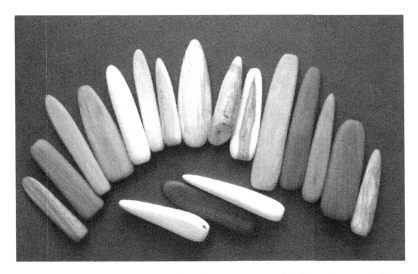

Chakra Sticks, copyright 2017 by Thomas Freese. Chakte Viga wood is the bright orange.

Chechen (CN)
Chechen enhances your spiritual strength to overcome internal conflicts. It allows you to see what you mask from yourself.

Cherry (CH)
LB: this wood neutralizes negativity and gives protection. AC: Cherry is grounding and tangible. It assists with the connection to present moments and grounds energy. Cherry helps you to bring in energy to utilize on this sphere called Earth. Cherry says, "I assist in bringing the energy to focus on the present and the now. I release the energy of worry and anxiety to restore harmony. I also readjust focus from the past and situations that have already occurred in this timeline and in others times as well."

Chestnut (CT)

Herbalists use Chestnut to help rid the body of toxins. A wand made of Chestnut can aid one to banish negativity and cleanse the home.

Clematis (CT)

Clematis is useful in magic to attain goals and achieve aspirations.

Cottonwood root (CW)

DE: Cottonwood burns bright and it is strong, but light. Trim cottonwood to create a small wand with a crystal mounted on it; this will provide a powerful healing combination.

AC: This wood brings a focus on the heart chakra and vascular health, helping us regain the balance and structure to physical life. Cottonwood root can improve blood flow and energy flow in the physical body "The human collective underestimates the balance of the heart energy. All of the highest vibration comes from joy and love which is the language of the heart. It is a relatively small organ in the body system, but its network of connection exists in the entire body. To survive the tissues must be connected to the blood and nutrient the body sends with love. This is also the path and constant connection to source energy. I assist in its maintenance.

Cottonwood Trees along the acequia, Albuquerque, Rio Grande Valley,
Photo by Thomas Freese

Crepe Myrtle (CM)

LB: Crepe Myrtle helps release stress and anger. This wood absorbs negativity. I see this wood working with the Chi energy flowing throughout your body. It creates a balancing and uplifting feeling.

AC: Crepe Myrtle energy affects the eyes and third eye chakra. It provides clarity and trust in connection with light. There is lots of white light with Crepe Myrtle. It raises the vibration of the body and aura and helps us access the angelic realm. Crepe Myrtle says, "You are a being of light and we wish for you to not only see this truth but feel it. We help you to bring light into the body and elevate the consciousness as well as the body/temple."

Cypress (CY)

Cypress can be used in magic for healing and longevity and is said to provide comfort and protection.

Cypress Tree, Cherokee Park, Louisville, KY, photo by Thomas Freese

Dogwood (DG)

DE: Strong energy! It almost gave me a headache at first and then it dissipated. When held long enough, dogwood can help with trance states, but make sure you are well protected. It opens to anyone. It also has healing abilities once it gets used to your energy.

LB: this wood helps us set our intentions, and leads us to see the joys of the manifestations of our purest of intentions. It challenges us to find the wisdom to set goals and see things from start to finish.

AC: Dogwood emphasizes metabolism and gland function. I feel energy in the thymus between the heart and throat chakras. It helps restore energetic and metabolic balance, and it can help with physical and emotional detoxing. Dogwood says, "The ecology of the physical being is critical to balance and energy transfer. If one part of the physicality is off balance the energy transmitted through the body cannot be in harmony. We balance all of the physical attributes with the energetic for smooth function in healers and other lightworkers. We can help you tap into ancient vibrations long lost to the human species to regain the harmony with Gaia and elemental energy."

Dogwood Tree in full springtime bloom. Photo by Thomas Freese

Ebony/Gaboon Ebony (GE)

AC: Gaboon Ebony provides balance, protection and grounding. This wood, and tree, feels very old energetically. I connect to pagan energy and something old and elemental with this. This wood makes powerful wands to be used for spells and breaking negativity. It hits upon the third eye chakra. Ebony provides a connection with the ancients, and with knowing and with the greater Self. Ebony says, "I work with the energy of change. How the energy shifts depends on the energy which you send out. I help you to connect to your inner truth and project your energy to help in the shift of you or your creations. I bring your memory of ancient energy and other dimensions."

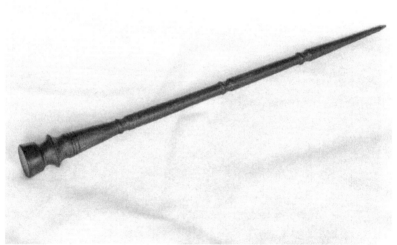

Hand crafted Gaboon Ebony wand by wood artist Robert Tuemler, in author Freese's private collection, 18 inches in length. Picture courtesy of Angela Hurd Greer.

Elder (ER)

Elder is the retreat of the Elder Mother, powerful matriarch of the hedgerows, woods and semi-wild places. She is the one who takes revenge on the despoilers of the countryside, and you cross her at your peril. It is said that you should never burn Elder wood on your fire, or the Elder Mother will burn your house down in retaliation. The wood of the Elder tree is especially highly charged magically and can add power to any magical undertaking. Along with Hazel, it is said to be one of the best woods for wands. It is seen as a threshold tree, guarding portals to other realms, and legend has it that it never gets struck by lightning. It is believed that an Elder stick will kill serpents and drive away robbers, and the twigs have been carried during wedding ceremonies for good luck. It can be used for protection or exorcism rituals, and to bring healing, prosperity or sleep. It is particularly good for making women more sexually attractive to men, and for increasing the male libido!

Elm (EM)
Elm can be used in any magic to do with love, whether romantic or any other kind.

Eucalyptus (EU)
LB: this wood helps with opening up feelings. It brings stability—emotionally, mentally and physically. It also helps with making decisions. This wood is good for grounding.

AC: Eucalyptus has the ability to strengthen the physical eyes as well as the ability to see and create manifestation. "The eyes and sight lines are where my focus and energy are aligned. To create a life you have to be able to see it. That is, to really see it not just think about it. I also assist in moving this sight from a version of a goal or daydream to one of reality in the physical world."

Fennel (FL)

Fennel wand was traditionally carried during classical times by the followers of Dionysius. It has commonly been used for purification rituals, and is said to be good for magic to do with protection and healing.

Fig (FG)
Fig is excellent for spells to do with romantic love and emotional balance. It is said to bring harmony between the sexes and to help with impotence and infertility. If placed above the door of your home it is said to ensure a safe return from a journey.

Fir (FR)
Fir is an immortal evergreen; it is protective of those who use it wisely.

Gorse (GS)
Gorse is strongly connected with the Sun and can be used in magic for money and protection. It is associated with new love and is said to feed the flames of passion! It is said to be effective when used in magic to do with fresh starts or new ventures.

Cultivated Grapevine at a winery, photo by Thomas Freese

Grapevine (GV)

Grapevine is held to be sacred in many cultures throughout the world, but holds a particularly important place in the Greek tradition as being the special plant of Dionysus. It has been used as a symbol of joy and exhilaration, but also of wanton lust and abandon. It is also symbolic of resurrection and transformation, and is useful in magic dealing with these themes.

Hackberry (HA)

LB: it is good for honesty, strength and truth; helps us to hold our own in the big world.

DE: I see that some part of the Hackberry had medicinal use and it was steeped in water for tea and was aromatic.

AC: Hackberry wood helps us to stay grounded. This tree is all about balance and structure. It can help release stress and anxiety into the earth and free the person wearing or touching it. Hackberry says, "Dream big and plant seeds for growth. Draw energy from the earth to remain balanced wherever you may travel. You are after all connected to it physically. Utilize the energy as well be present in each moment."

Hawthorn (HW)

Hawthorn, or May as it is also known, is excellent for magic to do with general happiness, because it dispels negative energy and strife and brings hope. It is useful for cleansing and purification, and is believed to ease enforced chastity and increase male potency. It is also said to bring good luck in fishing!

Good for matters relating to general happiness, hope, purification, cleansing and male potency. Also said to bring good luck in fishing!

Hazel (HZ)

Hazel is an exceptionally magical tree, as well as being extremely useful on the physical plane. It is best known for being the Celtic Tree of Wisdom and is said to bring luck, fertility, intelligence and inspiration. Together with Elder, it is said to be one of the best woods for wands. If you hang it in your window it will protect your house from lightning, and it is also supposed to help make wishes come true!

Heather (HR)
Heather is one of the classic woods to carry for good luck and protection, and for centuries it was almost indispensable as part of a bridal bouquet. It has traditionally been used in magic to bring rain, or to enhance beauty. Beloved by the Faeries, it can apparently open a portal from this world into the Faeries' realm. It is said to promote generosity of spirit and to bring a better awareness of others' needs. It also encourages passionate love, but, paradoxically, can also provide protection against violent assault, especially rape. Wearing the wood is said to bring a long life.

Hemlock (HE)
LB: this wood brings messages from the archangels. It sings their praise and brings healing to feelings of a broken heart. It helps us to feel the loving embrace of the archangels.
DE: If you stand or sit in a Hemlock grove then you can hear them sing with the wind. Hemlock still sings on if held during meditation. It soothes, calms and heals. Hemlock opens the heart chakra and then its energy flows to rest of body.
AC: Hemlock gracefully brings us reflection and gratitude. You can feel this energy in your soul core. Hemlock is also a cool energy. It brings physical healing to the intestinal area. Hemlock says, "In order to invite abundance and expansion into your world it is necessary to

look at life through the eyes and perception of gratitude. I assist in helping the humans to see what they value and move from a place of greed to a true place of acceptance and humbleness. I expand the idea of true gratitude. It is a deeply held appreciation for life, self, and the connection to like-minded, family, and others in your inner circle. Hold and cherish connection that inspires gratitude, and release the rest to incompatibility on an energetic level. Appreciate that which will create your ideal future."

Hickory (HC)
LB: This is a heavy, solid piece of wood. This wood brings strength and focus. Hickory tells me it is old and reliable. It helps bring ideas to fruition and helps to resolve challenges in your life.

AC: Hickory deals with balance, creation, and direction. It energizes the sacral chakra. It can help female health and possibly infertility. This comes from ideas as well as physical. "Passion for life and all its possibilities can be achieved relatively easily. Many humans struggle with this. I assist in aligning the sacral area with source energy and clearing energy that blocks a person from feeling such a connection. All energy experienced in a physical body of this nature is a direct link and memory to being in nonphysical energy. I assist with reconnecting it in order to draw upon it to create the same in your own life. I also strengthen the balance of kundalini energy as well as helping propel the energy in the direction you have chosen. Draw upon this energy when in need. It is my honor to assist."

Holly (HO)
LB: This wood brings a high energy, grounding us and reducing stress and anxiety.

DE: Holly would make excellent divining rods. You would need two thin sticks about two feet long. Hold one in each hand out in front of you. They will cross, making an "X" when you have found what you are looking for. You must have the intention for that which you search.

AC: Holly brings purity and absolutions. This wood has the ability to cleanse away energy from emotional trauma and other events that have been trapped and which need to be cleared in this lifetime. I feel its energy in the heart chakra but it is different than the others. It feels like my heart is going to burst! I see rainbows of energy and colors. Holly projects all spectrums of light and energy. Holly says, "I assist in transmuting energy and releasing signatures of trauma and fear. To find yourself you must release the energy trapped that is interfering with the ability to connect to your higher perspectives and healing."

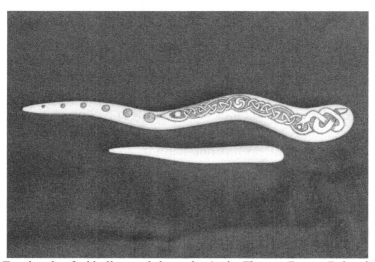

Two handcrafted holly wands by author/artist Thomas Freese. Below is a 6 ½ inch long holly wand with gentle curves. Above is the author/Freese's Celtic Dragon serpentine wand, 17 inches long. Picture courtesy of Angela Hurd Greer.

Honeysuckle (HY)
AC: brings purity, cleansing, and evolution. It also connects to some fairy energies. Honeysuckle sends gentle waves of white light through one's entire body when holding it. It also positively affects the third eye chakra, boosting spiritual connection and oneness. Honeysuckle says, "I work with the vibration of faith and cleansing; that is faith in Self and faith in Spirit. I bring connection, unity, and a sense of belonging. These vibrations assist you to ascend to higher planes of connection and information. I assist with the connection to higher beings of light and universal consciousness."

Ipe (IP)
Ipe draws from the elements earth and water. It is used for healing, protection, growth and luck rituals. Achieve success with this wood as your companion. Excellent for renewal spells.

Iroko (IK)
Iroko is widely revered in African culture connecting the sky and the earth. It is also used in ship-building and strongly related to Neptune and the energies of the sea.

Ivy (IV)
Ivy is good for love magic, especially if it relates to fidelity or constancy, and is said to promote faithful friendship. It is useful for anything to do with protection and healing and can be used for binding spells. It is said to provide protection from intoxication!

Jobillo (JO)
LB: Jobillo helps to balance the chakras and works well with Reiki healing as a tool for releasing stress, tension. It helps with physical health and mental clarity. I see this

wood associated with the color pink which means love, loving yourself, loving others and forgiveness.

AC: Jobillo energy touches the area between the third eye and crown chakras. Its emphasis is on clarity and focus, aligning thoughts and clearing mental clutter. It provides a minor positive effect on the ear chakras as well. Jobillo could help with polarity imbalances and hyperactivity. Jobillo says, "Human life is full of much noise and clutter and the ideal would be to move toward a greater simplicity. I assist you in clearing away noises, to simplify and focus on thoughts that will bring you to your next step instead of the swirling energy of scatter. I help maintain the energetic balance of the brain quadrants and maintain symmetrical flow. In order to not feel overwhelmed and stay in the frequency of joy mental clarity is a necessity."

Katalox (KX)
Katalox is grounding yet insightful and it can aid in balancing strong emotions to clear your path to understanding.

Kingwood (KW)
AC: Kingwood provides an overwhelming sense of peace. It is also a cool energy. It connects to third eye chakra but more about perception than anything else. It emphasizes the idea of seeing beauty in the everyday things around you. Kingwood says, "I assist you in maintaining focus and perception. It is my great honor and privilege to provide a sense of comfort and joy, and moving perceptions and energy back to what is versus what is not changeable. You are able to see beauty in each moment if you choose."

Kou (KO)
Kou draws off the elements of fire and wind. This is a neutral wood, preferring neither white nor dark Magic, and

has good defensive energy. Koa represents the full circle of birth, destruction and rebirth.

Lacewood (LC)
Lacewood is full of positive energy, lucky, and useful in divination.

Larch (Tamarack) (LA)
LB: this wood helps us to provide for the needs of others. It brings a strength but with humility. It encourages us to find happiness with those who share.
DE: Larch represents journeying and creativity. It helps you to relax and is good for meditation.
AC: With Larch, the focus is in the third eye. This wood helps us with intuition and self-trust. Larch assists the empath to remain aware and objective—concerning energy and the exchange of it with other people, places, and objects. It allows the holder to align with their higher self. Larch says, "You cannot create or live the life you desire if you cannot trust your discernment or choices. Align with what you know without judgment."

Laurel Negro (LN)
LB: I see Laurel Negro wood working in conjunction with heart and lungs. It also helps with memory and opening up the third eye. This is a good strong solid piece of wood.
AC: Laurel Negro connects to the root chakra and tailbone. It helps with balance and structural support, and can help alleviate back pain. Laurel Negro moves balance and trust in Divine Source through the root chakra and lower back. Laurel Negro says, "There is never a time for you to fear the unknown circumstances in human perceptions. You are always supported in even the most seemingly dire of circumstances. We help you to translate

the energy of trust to the body and mind for an overall feeling of being supported and grounded."

Leopard Wood (LP)

LB: this tree and its energy will tolerate many things. It absorbs negativity and puts out positive energy—use it as a generator. Leopard wood is strong and stable and in tune with nature. It helps us with emotional, mental, physical and spiritual growth. It collects energy from the sun, and assists us in clarifying our ideas and thoughts. Its energy is similar to faceted quartz crystals.

AC: Leopard wood positively affects both the solar plexus and all of the physical body. This wood promotes healthy tissue growth and healthy cell regeneration. It unravels emotions tied to cellular malformation, and it could greatly assist cancer patients. Leopard wood says, "The human body can alter tissues which have been previously based on poor nutrients and emotional vibrations that are not aligned with harmony and joy. I can assist the body to realign. This vibration can return physical tissues to their pristine forms."

Lignum Vitae (LV)

This wood has a profoundly positive energy. The overall energy of the wood can be summed up as the power and strength of goodness. Its strong connections with the sun, Jupiter, and luck energy make it an ideal tool for any worker of positive magic. The energy about the wood is very healing, in both physical and spiritual matters. The energies within the wood would also be excellent for divining information from far away as well as close to home. This wood represents the end of strife and the beginning of a new, positive, cycle.

Linden (LI)
Linden is commonly known as Lime. Linden is said to be protective and can be useful in magic to do with love and luck. It is associated with immortality and is said to promote peaceful sleep.

Macassar Ebony (ME)
LB: this energy is ancient and is grounded. This wood repels negativity, and provides us with strength and power.
DE: Macassar Ebony works with all chakras to clear, balance, and realign.
AC: Macassar Ebony initiates emotional flexibility and provides physical healing to connective tissues. The energy of this wood enhances a person's ability to cope and move forward through, and leave behind, difficult situations. It has a very intense vibration of perseverance. I pick up the energy in my calves which is specific to working with the ebb and flow of energy as well as connection to physical life. Macassar Ebony says, "Through your walk in a physical life you will be handed many challenges and lessons you have established for yourself to grow and evolve a greater understanding of life experiences and some are related to karmic situations as well. I bring the energy of flexing to move gracefully through these experiences and assist in peaceful transitions."

Magnolia (MO)
AC: Magnolia energizes ambition, thoughts, dreams, goals, and brings dream ideas into the physical world. Its energy connects to the back of the head in the third eye chakra. Magnolia says, "What you desire in your life will not magically fall into your lap without the alignment of vibration. I assist in this process of aligning the dream world and physical world's achievements. Connecting energy, actions, joy, and the magic of dreaming will bring you what you wish to create."

Mahogany (MG)

LB: this wood is like a beacon of light, helping others to find their way. It awakens the light within our hearts. It encourages us to speak up and find strength through generosity.

DE: Mahogany can help correct minor vision issues; its effectiveness is with the third eye chakra. It can help curb appetite if carried continuously on one's person. It also ameliorates sleep issues if you sleep with it under your pillow.

AC: Mahogany teaches us how to overcome fear and other three-dimensional emotions and energy. Its power is in our root chakra. Mahogany says, "As you evolve and grow in your perceptions and vibration it is necessary to start at the beginning. You have within you a great deal of animal and primal emotions from the early days as a physical species. You see these every day on your news channels and other outlets. It is the root of all destructive behavior and emotions and part of the ascension process. It is necessary to experience and understand these primal instincts and feelings. You must have a great scope of understanding to be able to master yourself as well as your responses. I assist in helping you move through these emotions and to develop a greater level of understanding of these vibrations of fear, hate, and jealousy and so on. All are forms of fear but distinctly different for the one experiencing them. I also assist in releasing and transmuting these emotions for those that utilize my energy."

Makore (MK)

LB: this wood shows us that good things are all around us. Although it is an old tree, it gives much strength and helps us to be grounded. It facilitates communication with all animals.

DE: For Makore, create a point, as for a wand, to direct beautiful healing energy. Focus with intention, and add a few crystals to strengthen the energy.

AS says this wood activates the solar plexus, clearing negative energy and establishing overall vitality. It helps you to create healthy boundaries and set limits. It also cuts etheric cords that attach you to the past and others energy who are not connecting in a wholesome manner. Makore says, "Trees share the soil in a healthy manner most of the time. We do have species of invasive trees much as some humans do—that will utilize all resources only for themselves. Notice those trees end up alone or in groups where greed consumes them much as they consumed others. It is necessary to interact with others. I will assist the holder in balancing their give and take with energy to remain balanced and in line with their thoughts."

Maple (MA)

LB: this wood leads us down the road less traveled, to discover new ideas and concepts and in the process find our inner peace. It provides us with a do-over for our life through dispelling fears and spurring us on to live life as our soul intended it to be.

DE: Maple wood is a storyteller. It is happiest when near water, even a glass of water! But sitting on the banks of a lake or by a gentle stream increases its power. Maple can help strengthen one's intuitive power.

AC: Maple highlights adaptability and evolutions, and it connects to the sacral chakra. Maple can be effective for psychic protection and releasing outside energy. It is helpful for empaths in particular. Maple says, "While all sentient beings are one some carry energy that is harmful for those who have low frequencies or the inability to deflect energy that harms them. I assist in not allowing those outside energies into the soul core. This keeps the energetic mission separate from all those in the physical presence, and does not allow a human to be invaded, depleted or harmed by energy from the outside."

Soft Maple Tree in Autumn Colors photo by
Thomas Freese

Mesquite (MQ)

LB: it has a heavier energy, a grounded feeling. It brings the wisdom of ancestors, possibly Native American. It gives a healing energy and is connected with astral travel.

DE: Mesquite helps one to relax.

AC: Mesquite highlights the energy of our eyes and of sight. It helps with healing of physical eyesight and helping you cope with what you don't wish to see and acknowledge. Mesquite says, "It is a terrifying journey for humans to see beyond levels of that they are given by society. It is an even more frightening journey to see what and who you are. Most don't dare to walk this path which is unfortunate for the energy of the collective. In order to change, you must be able to see what is without eyes of judgment. What do you see and what do you want to be? How must these align in order to get there? Have the courage to see and life will be a brighter experience."

Mimosa (MS)

AC: Mimosa provides immunity and cellular strength. It establishes a connection physically to the nerve tissue and spinal column; this allows one to stand peacefully in your strength, and not allowing your energy to be "fed" on. It is effective for empaths to shield their energy. Mimosa says, "When connecting with humans it is my great duty to teach empowerment and love. Expressing unconditional love comes from an appreciation of self and the grace that comes from fully embracing it. As I share the energy with the collective of this planet I pass imprints of love and compassion, and feeling completely supported."

Monterillo (MT)

This tree draws from the elements of earth and fire and represents strength, courage, and determination. Although it is used for defensive magic, there is a dangerous power to this wood that can unleash deadly curses if wielded to do so.

Mulberry (MB)

LB: is strong and powerful, and watches people. Its energy is analytical and it promoted logical thinking. Mulberry's energy connects to the heart chakra. It won't "settle for less" and reminds us that the "eyes are the window to our soul."

AC: this tree's energy moves through soul core at the navel chakra, reconnecting timelines and Akashic/karmic fractures in your energy. It helps to heal past life issues. Mulberry says, "Past present and future are all aligned and not separate. In order to feel whole, you much align all energy that you are a part of. I will assist your energy in this task so long as the will is also aligned with the purpose."

Myrtle (MY)

Myrtle helps by balancing the energy in ourselves or in our situations. It has an honest energy that requires forthright intentions in your work.

Narra (NR)

Narra is powerful like ebony, yet a little more difficult to control because its energy constantly shifts. Narra is more feminine than its cousin and can be a potent healer in the right hands.

Nettles (NT)

Nettles main use is in exorcism and the casting out of evil spirits, but it is also useful in magic for protection and healing. It is said to promote lust!

Oak (OK)

LB: this wood represents the fairy realm, doesn't sweat the small stuff, optimistic, playful and childlike.
DE: Oak instantly calms and helps us relax. It has a feel-good energy.
AC: Oak is all about focusing intention and aligning that focus. It helps narrow the mental chatter down to a single thought and intention and then multiplies that intention into the universe. Oak gives healing energy with lots of pink and silver colors therein. It helps to boost the throat chakra and encourages us to speak our truth.

Olive (OL)

LB: this tree helps us to right the wrongs of the world, to let our lives change to put away any soul ugliness and replace it with love—for all of mankind.

DE: Olive leaves are medicinal, not to eat or drink, but used on wounds mixed with mud.

AC: Olive stimulates the crown chakra. It gives polarity balance and expansion of the energy column in the body. There is lots of white light with olive wood. Olive says, "Through the centuries we have witnessed a great amount of change on this planet, and we hope to see humankind come back into connection with nature and the wisdom, peace, and harmony with life restored. We assist you as a physical reminder and help rebalance the magnetics of the body with the changes moving through the physical planes. These times are a great journey through energetic changes. We are here to bring the frequencies required to maintain your grounded connection with us and the elements of earth to expand information that passes through the body for protection, peace, and what you humans would refer to as sanity."

Old Osage Orange, Henderson, Kentucky Photo by Thomas Freese

Osage orange (OO)

LB: this wood is tough, dependable and resilient. Helps boost pride—I can hang with the best. It is also good for astral travel.

DE: Osage orange is the tree of knowledge. It cleanses Earth's energy more than most and can do the same for humans—kind of like dialysis.

AC: Osage orange highlights ancient wisdom and accomplishment. It touches us between the heart chakra and solar plexus. This energy moves straight through the soul core, aligning lifetimes and wisdom in a peaceful flow and progression. Osage orange helps to heal old wounds and karmic ties. Osage orange says, "Much like the rings in my structure your experiences through lifetimes have created layers of your perceptions of reality. The higher the levels of perception of circumstances the more rings of experience the soul has gathered. Be patient with souls still beginning to gather their rings."

Paduak (PK)

LB: Paduak helps to bring you out of depressive thoughts. The angels with this wood say 'a giggle a day keeps the gloomies away'. It repels negativity and keeps you protected."

AC: Paduak accentuates the top part of the throat chakra. It focuses on singing and clearing the way for higher vibrations of sound and wisdom. It would be good to have during public speaking, as it helps one in honoring truth and aligning with communication. Paduak says, "I offer my assistance in the arts of communication, language, and song. For many peoples song and speaking were methods of passing histories, sacred traditions, and knowledge to the next generations. I inspire the energies of reconnection with lost information and expansion of those only just created."

Paperbark Tree (PT)

AC: Paperbark Tree affects dual placement energy wise on the body. First, it affects the third eye chakra in order to give clear insights and also psychic growth. Second, the paperbark tree focuses on the sacral chakra to help us own and accept truth. Paperbark tree says, "To know your worth you must fully accept your own value and stand in a place of joy. I not only help you hold the energy of joy but also allow you to see beyond what you know as truth and connect you to what you already know as an experienced soul."

Celtic zoomorphic interlace crafted from the Paperbark Tree
Artwork and photo by Thomas Freese

Pau Rosa (PA)

LB: is good for grounding our energies, bringing calm and peace. This tree energy helps bring like-minded people together, helping to touch and heal our souls. Pau Rosa can also help bring forgiveness related to our past life experiences.

AC: Pau Rosa affects the heart chakra and heart health, by moving vibrations of love and aligning higher self with Divine Source. Pau Rosa says, "Building walls against the notion of emotional pain can be most detrimental to overall physical health. I assist in realigning the energy of your heart to its spiritual residence with vibrations of love and purity."

Pear (PR)

LB: it represents the fairy and angelic realm. It brings balance (yin/yang) and helps us to be present in all situations.

DE: Holding pear wood I felt instantly thirsty. It likes water and can help a person drink and process the water they drink. Pear helps to balance the chakras.

AC: Pear points to speeding the path to personal growth and fast tracks the spiritual journey and energetic evolution. It should be used energetically or worn in moderation. There is a time for fast growth and yet a time to slow the pace. Pear tree encourages the shifts to become more rapid and allows for all released or suppressed emotions to be moved quickly. Its energy is felt in the psychic centers of the face; that is, in the eyes, nose, ears, and taste palette. Pear says, "I move along my growth cycle quickly and encourage the same energy in my presence. I can assist in moving energy that is stagnant, and with releasing multitudes in a short time span. Not all energy can be moved rapidly, and I can assist in halting the process but only for brief periods of time. Change is consistent, necessary and, expected in physicality."

Persimmon, American (PM)

AC: American persimmon connects to the just above the sacral chakra and provides alignment to child-like purity. It works to construct codes of joy and harmony. This tree says, "Incorporating the idealism of youth and seeing life from a mystical and play-like stance can elevate the entire body, mind and spirit. I bring the energy of the elves and other nature spirits to interact from cellular memory in the body. Remember a time of play and fantasy. Remembering to play as a youth is a state of mind."

Persimmon, Asian (PMA)

LB: This wood has the heaviest energy of all the woods. It feels like male energy. This is a good wood for motivation and staying focused. I feel this would be a great piece for Reiki healing and balancing Chakras.

AC: Asian Persimmon focuses on love, healing and remembrance. Its emphasis is with the heart chakra. It provides healing of old wounds that have created a blockage to receiving love and disconnecting any memory or idea that the heart should be protected from receiving love. "It is common to have the heartbreak emotion in the physical form. All manners of life feel this. The animals grieve and feel this as well as the humans. I bring the energy to heal wounds, the feelings of disconnect for that is what they are. When the feeling of rejection or loss is experienced it is, in fact, an illusion that you are no longer loved or cared for by Divine Source. This causes a feeling of great despair. But you are not alone and you are never separate from God. It isn't a possibility in the intricate connection of energy. I assist in reconnecting and healing to align with receiving love."

(Asian) Persimmon Root (PMR)

LB: I feel this wood connects to the angel and fairy Realms. Wish upon a star and the angels and fairies will help fulfill your desires. This is a good wood for healing—emotionally, mentally physically and spiritually. I like this because of its ability to bring bonding and healing to relationships.

AC: This provides grounding and a balance of earth energy. It activates the chakras in the soles of the feet. It also expands kundalini energy as well as connection to the earth grids. "In your life experience will inevitably come times of upheaval, shock, and other events that sever your connection to the earth and the stability that being grounded brings to you. I rebalance this connection as well as the connection to your core foundation and trust in yourself and Source. Being in the present moment is critical for peace and elevation to the next stage. I assist the humans in this critical stage"

These are Asian Persimmon roots dug out by my neighbor. His tree died and he dug the roots out to make space for a new tree. Folks don't know that root has bark; although tough to work with, roots make wonderful wands—people love the energy! Picture by Thomas Freese

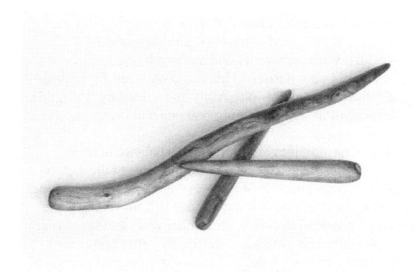

Three wands crafted from Asian Persimmon root. These came from a neighbor's persimmon tree. Wand lengths are 5 3/4, 7 ½ and 14 inches. Photo courtesy Angela Hurd Greer.

Pine (PN)

Pine is excellent for healing, it is said that just its presence in the sick room can speed recovery. It has traditionally been used for fertility and money spells and considered to be useful for magic involving change or shapeshifting. It protects against all forms of negativity and can be used in exorcism rituals.

Pine Tree photo by Thomas Freese

Pink Ivory (PI)

LB: this wood embraces us and helps us to overcome fears
and dispel anger. It teaches us to release with love and
forgiveness.

DE: Pink Ivory is strong with lots of endurance against the elements. It is perfect as a wand and stands alone.

AC: Pink Ivory is a teacher for us, and helps us connect with memory. Pink Ivory serves to reconnect us with our past life and also to cosmic knowledge in the present. This wood assists your tapping into what you know but are not aware of. Pink Ivory says, "As you have traveled lifetimes and dimensional planes of energy you have acquired a great deal of knowledge and skills. I help you to reconnect with them to utilize the information of skills in this present time. This reestablishes a connection with timelines and a feeling of being complete. In reality you always are aware, but as you are often disconnected to different aspects of yourself it is difficult to feel it. When you are in unison with your aspects you are able to connect on a much more distinct level to yourself and your goals."

Plum (PM)

LB: it sends us on a mission to find the warmth of others, which will, in turn, warm our soul. This tree teaches us to bring generosity and kindness to others.

DE: Plum likes people; it carries the ability to communicate as well as helping to heal whatever ails one. Before Earth's soil was contaminated, ancient people boiled the bark as a healing drink, although this is not safe anymore. They also burned this wood in their lodge as its smoke helped to heal.

AC: Plum provides overall balance and reestablishment of emotions and chakras. Feel the energy all through the body—it just brings a wash of peacefulness. Plum says, "The human collective, in general, has lost touch with nature and itself in the process. I bring to you the energy to reestablish this connection as well as the one with yourself. I assist in balancing the body energetically and rebalancing the mind, bringing you to thoughts of a place of peace. To move forward in your evolution you must be able to remain in balance while processing energy. I assist with this balance and bring about the space in which to find it."

Poculi (PC)

Poculi is a feminine wood, and it creates romance and harmony. It is good for healing.

Poplar (PP)

LB: this wood encourages thoughtfulness, and helps us to see through our insecurities. It reminds us to see through the muck and detach from negativity; we can confidently take charge of situations.

DE: Poplar gains strength and happiness when paired with crystals. It needs that freedom of not being mixed with other woods or put away in a dark place or sack.

AC: The focus with Poplar wood is language and communication. Literally—the energy is in the tongue. Poplar assists the holder in speech, crafting language and effective communication. Poplar tree says, "The ability to communicate is an art form. Humans hear what they feel and not what is stated as it was often intended. I will assist in the ability to communicate in varying levels to be heard as intended with whoever is being communicated. This allows the holder to trust the words they choose and craft the correct verbiage for the situation."

A wonderful and practical source for wood that is already dried and essentially stable is architectural salvage. Here is native Tulip Poplar harvested in the late 1700s and part of a building for 150 years. Note the old square cut nail in the lower right. Photo by Thomas Freese

Purpleheart (PH)

AC: Purpleheart provides grounding and connection with nature and earth energy, and the emphasis is with the Earth Star chakra (located below the feet). This wood can help with anxiety and trauma release. It also helps with balance and connection to physical elements. Purpleheart says, "The earth is your physical home and the energy provided by it is essential to your balance energetically. I wish for you to stay connected to Gaia and all the information and reassurance she and the other earth energies bring to you. These energies are essential to grounding and the ability to accept situations on a physical plane to let them go and move forward."

Redbud (RB)

LB: it needs to be included, doesn't want to feel left out. It promotes curiosity, strength and perseverance. It is a peacemaker.

AC: Redbud tree wishes to see joyful energy spread throughout the planet! It assists in raising heart energy and heart chakra. It may also be used to assist in detoxing parasites from the body. Redbud says, "Sacred is the heart that is filled with joy."

Redheart (Chakte Coc) (RH)

This wood draws off the element of earth and water. It contains an overall bright and carefree energy. It is an excellent wood for those seeking to be able to focus more on the here and now rather than dwelling on past or possible future events. It allows one to follow their whims, set aside their fears, and move their life in an overall positive direction. It does not distract one from real threats, but rather removes the fear and doubt that can cloud our judgment and make us imagine things worse than they may actually be. This wood will aid a person in finding their personal truth, free of self-deception. Redheart is a resilient wood that is good at both conducting and holding energy.

Rhododendron (RD)

Rhododendron is said to help with the process of focusing on knowledge and enhances one's awareness of enemies.

Rose (RO)

Rose is most strongly associated with charms to do with romantic love, but it is also excellent for emotional healing. It is said to bring luck and protection and can be used to aid divination and enhance psychic power.

Rosemary (RM)

Rosemary has always been used for remembrance, not just of people or past events but also to encourage learning and increase divinatory powers. It is excellent for magic concerning healing and purification, love and lust and is said to bring peaceful sleep and to enhance youthfulness. It is strongly protective and can be used for exorcism.

Rosewood (RW)

LB: this tree opens up our solar plexus to free our emotions! It shows us how to accept our feelings and open up to love and forgiveness.

DE: I see Rosewood high on a hill, as it watched a forest fire destroy trees around it, but this tree was not harmed. It still feels sad, still grieving for the loss of all others below. Rosewood says, "People took only what they wanted of me and left the rest. I am happy to be this small piece, I am making a difference... but so much of me was wasted when I could have been of greater use."

AC: Rosewood gives us structure and stability. Its energy is felt in the shoulders. Rosewood says, "Many times spirit can separate from the body partially or fully. I help the bearer come back into the physical structure and reconnect to the soul while still fully inhabiting the body. There is a deep remembrance for some of the energy of the universe while not being segregated as an individual in human form. I help to pull scattered and uncooperative energy back into the center to improve the connection to the now and appreciate the ability to be unique. I assist in rearranging the feeling of being scattered—fractured, or disconnected—to stability and focus. I also help the soul to remember the purpose of being incarnate to promote cooperation and minimize struggle for the bearer."

Rowan (RN)

Rowan is very protective, especially against lightning and evil witchery, and can be useful in healing. It is said to increase psychic powers and bring power and success. It is allegedly the best wood to use if dowsing for metal. It is also the traditional choice for Druid's staffs.

The characteristic "mitten" shape of the Sassafras tree leaves, photo by Thomas Freese

Sassafras (SF)

LB: this holds many secrets and it teaches and helps. It is no-nonsense and gives a very mystical feeling of protection.

DE: As I held Sassafras, I could see my aura brighten and feel my chakras clearing and balancing. It can help one journey during meditation.

AC: Sassafras wood affects our knees and thus highlights movement and growth. It can help with manifestation and personal growth. Sassafras says, "In order to travel through what you know in life you must be able to visualize and decide what you desire. Goals and dreams do not travel in a straight line path. For you to achieve anything or be who you wish to become you have to have vision. Develop the ability to daydream. It's where you reconnect the bridge of possibility and potential within yourself."

Sea Grape (SG)
AC: Sea Grape offers structure, balance and calm. Its energy connects to the navel area and pulls emotional and physical balance to center. Its work is with healing energy related to bones and structure. Sea Grape says, "I assist you in building your framework in life. This relates to calm perception and the physical health needed to achieve it. I work on a vibration, geometric, and cell level to help bring energy and well-being to center. I am the tree of life." This tree is a powerful physical healer, and it might be effective for those who have nerve and genetic disorders.

Sequoia (Redwood) (SQ)
LB: don't underestimate the power of this tree, looks can be deceiving. The overlaying energy is easy going, but don't ruffle my feathers! It provides protection.
DE: Sequoia feels good, and happy. I can see a tree with birds on the branches singing. It brings joy and sunshine as it is held.
AC: Sequoia represents receiving and releasing. It helps to maintain the balance of energy transfer. Its power comes into our hands and feet. It keeps the balance of energy entering the body as to that of what's being released. Sequoia says, "Peace exists in balance. Healing and harmony exist in balance. I assist in this plane to maintain it."

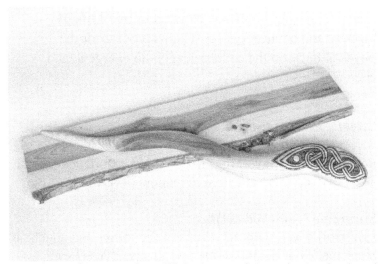

Two pieces of Dawn Redwood/lightning struck Sequoia. One is a board cut from the logs of the local Dawn Redwood lightning struck tree, and the other is a serpentine wand wood burned with Celtic knots. Picture courtesy of Angela Hurd Greer.

Shedua (SD)

Shedua draws from the element of earth. This is a neutral wood that works well with the mind. It is excellent for healing and charms.

Snakewood (SW)

LB: Snakewood is strong and sturdy and this wood prevents you from procrastinating. It is deep rooted into Mother Earth. It's a good wood for those with back issues. It also takes away stress and worries. I feel this wood represents longevity with relationships.

AC: Snakewood affects the body in the liver area, at the solar plexus chakra and meridian. This force is less energetic and more physical. Snakewood assists with detoxification and purity. It helps with cleansing the toxins from tissues down to cellular levels, and aids in the liver processes of cleansing the body. Snakewood says,

"Optimal physical health is required to live a life of purpose and connection. I assist this process for the physical body on the cellular level both energetic and chemical."

Sweet Chestnut (SC)
Sweet Chestnut is also known as Spanish chestnut. It is said to be useful in all workings to do with romantic love, and is also believed to be effective in matters of fertility.

Suriname Ironwood (SI)
LB: works well with the realms of the fairies and angels. It helps make our dreams come true. It says, "Yes I can!"
AC: Suriname Ironwood connects with the energy of the pineal gland. It is a high vibration wood. It helps the physical body to hold and accept higher vibrations and dimensional connection. This tree has strong ties to angelic and mythic realms. Suriname Ironwood says, "I encourage you to BE—nothing more and nothing less. Just to align and BE. There is great promise in stillness and acceptance."

Sycamore (SY)
LB: the feeling is stoic. It helps restore memory and clarity. It is a medicinal wood to help with healing.
DE: Sycamore helps to open people's understanding—their energetic comprehension. I can feel the heart, throat, and third eye chakras responding.
AC: Sycamore represents unity of mind and thoughts. It assists in raising our overall vibration, with the crown chakra most affected. It also balances the voice of the ego with that of inner knowing. Sycamore says, "Awareness of thought is the key to Ascension."

Thomas Freese inside large Sycamore Trunk photo by Patricia McQuade

Tambootie (TB)

AC: This wood works on the throat chakra, with a very warm and nurturing energy. It brings a sense of encouragement and warmth. This could be an effective healer for depression and low self-worth. Tambootie says, "I assist humanity in its evolution through connecting to compassion, that is, compassion of self and of others with whom you share energy. I help with healing and moving energy with support and encouragement to unravel energy through all space and time."

Teak (TK)

Teak draws off the element of water. It is a feminine wood used for defensive work. It seeks a creative companion and one in touch with nature. Teak evokes the cleansing energy of the sea. Excellent for protection spells.

Thistle (TH)
Thistle is believed to be very strongly protective and is used in magic for the breaking of curses. It is said to bring strength and to aid healing.

Tiger Wood (TW)
AC: Tiger Wood energizes one's focus and ambition. It touches upon the solar plexus chakra. With Tiger wood, you get clarity and a laser sharp focus. It also helps to minimize scattered thoughts and energy. Its etheric color is orange and yellow. As much as it promotes focus it also allows creativity to merge. Tiger Wood says, "Time is not linear…at times it is necessary to focus your attention in that direction to achieve and accomplish goals and life missions that you sent before yourself."

Tulipwood (TW)
LB: this wood brings luck, helps with the release of pain—emotional, physical, mental and sexual. It can assist us in seeing past lives and help others too along the path of healing—giving us the strength to carry on.
DE: Tulipwood when held to my third eye, I saw beautiful multicolored rays of light similar to the colors in the wood. It brings us energy.
AC: Tulipwood brings us creativity, adventure, and joy. This is another that inspires creativity, but this is in the form of experience and travel—adding stories and experience to the life line. Tulipwood says, "When the soul returns to the creator at the end of a lifetime it is my goal to inspire the humans to experience the sights and sounds available in the physical or etheric realms. I can assist you in safe travels both in the body and those traveled on the astral planes."

Vermelha (VM)

This wood seeks a strong companion. It draws off the elements of fire and earth. Vermelha creates energy and balance, and it is excellent for protection spells.

Black Walnut (BW)

LB: it has a friendly energy, sees the good in all, and likes to help the underdog.

DE: Walnut is strong. I keep seeing Native Americans. They used walnut wood for carrying people and they made frames for teepees and lodges. Elemental spirits love to find holes in this wood to create homes or safe places.

AC: Black Walnut gives us humor and laughter. It directs energy to our throat chakra, helping with expansion of energy and encouraging the ability to laugh. Black Walnut says, "Find humor in situations that otherwise might cause your demise. Laughter is known to be the best medicine, and it is a statement of truth. When you physically laugh it lightens your energy and allows whatever negative you were storing to be released with the change in vibration. Extended periods of laughter can become painful as too much of the stored heavy energy leaves the body too quickly. Laugh often and laugh fully. Life is not meant to always be serious. Laughter leads to the lightness of heart and soul."

Wenge (pronounced WEN-gee) (WG)

LB: this wood has childlike energy and it helps you to see things as though through the eyes of a child. Wenge accentuates independence and it helps you to complete things from start to finish--putting forth your best effort. It boosts creativity while also helping you to put things together in a logical and direct manner."

AC: Wenge tunes into the solar plexus, releasing negativity and providing psychic protection. It can ward off evil spirits. Wenge says, "I offer to you the ability to stand in sacred space and help create hallowed ground. I offer peace, protection and cleansing."

Willow (WW)

LB: this wood is underestimated—people don't recognize its durability. It helps us to withstand stress, to step back, assess situations and then to take action.

AC: Willow tree and wood enhances the glands and general function of the body and metabolism. It is useful for resetting organ vibration to an optimal level. Willow energy connects to the thymus and promotes general wellbeing. Willow says, "I bring to you the balance of physical attributes. For life to be lived to its utmost potential it is critical to have a healthy body to take the soul along its adventures. My primary concern is to see the human collective fuel their bodies and maintain health to live the journey the utmost quality."

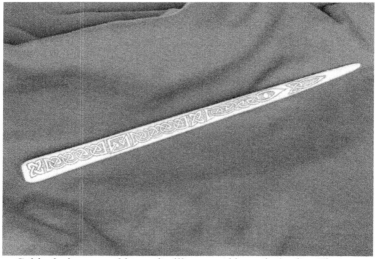

Celtic designs wood burned willow wand by artist/author Thomas Freese, 17 inches long. Picture courtesy of Angela Hurd Greer.

Yellowheart (YH)

LB: helps us to laugh, love life, take chances and get out of our own way. It assists us in releasing fears and knowing that anything is possible!

AC: Yellow heart sends energy to the chakra at the eyes. It clears insights and provides vision. Yellowheart opens imagination and intuition. It is good for writers, and pencils made from this wood can help move beyond writer's block. Yellowheart says, "In order to see clearly it is important to align your thoughts in silence and truth. Information obtained from this space will offer a greater understanding as well as clear the energy that prevents you from finding it. I help this process by aligning the creativity to the intuition with the divine."

English Yew tree, photo by Thomas Freese

Yew (YT)
LB: This wood feels like an old spirit, but has very light
energy. I feel this is connected to the upper world Spirit
teachers—for shamanic journeying—that is, teachers who
are human-like, animal-like, and god-like and so on. This is
a great piece of wood for calming, meditation and

grounding. If you feel negative and you are holding this wood, it would absorb this energy from you, release it and then the wood would be recharged.

AC: Yew attends to the third eye chakra and magic. Yew helps with altering negative perception into one of wonder and awe. It helps awaken curiosity, a quest for information and returns us to a childlike energy. "My greatest joy is to provide clarity of thought and to invite the alteration of negative perception into one of light and harmony with the energy of spirit as well as the earth. Joyful energy propels the energy of creation forward. I wish to see all of humanity remain in balance with joy.

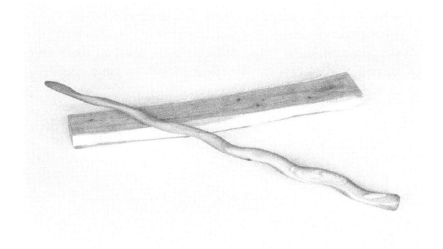

Taxus shrub/yew spiral wand and small log section from the same yew tree. Picture courtesy of Angela Hurd Greer.

Zebrawood (ZW)

LB: Brings strength and abundance, and a strong regard for life. It teaches us to withstand the tests of time. Its energetic help connects to the liver and the kidneys. It assists us to connect to celestial beings and for astral travel. AC: Zebrawood activates the chakra at the feet, stimulating kundalini energy and providing grounding. It connects to ancient wisdom and vibrations in the earth that can promote enlightenment. Zebrawood says, "I assist you to connect to the ancient energies of wisdom and oneness. I can help you commune with the spirits of animals and mineral kingdoms for information and energy channeling purposes."

Ziricote (ZC)

Ziricote is a masculine wood. It is a powerful wood that delves into the deeper levels of the mind, and it is an essential companion as a protector. But it can also be dangerous in the wrong hands. Used for reversal spells and dispelling dark magic—excellent for protection work

The Whole Living Tree versus a Piece of Wood

A piece of wood might appear at first glance to be an inanimate chunk of something dead…but the surface view of things I would consider to be misleading. In our Western mechanistic worldview we so often devalue the spiritual element of objects, while focusing on a reductionist set of observations. "This was a part of a living tree, and now it's just a remnant of its one time glory. There is nothing here of any use, other than for firewood, a chunk to carve or as a doorstop or garden mulch."

Perhaps we can question these limited assumptions and take in the wider view—that all things carry vibrant energy, that objects have a history, and that the sum of the whole imbues each part with the characteristics and power of the complete organism. In traditional Chinese medicine, the whole is fully represented in each part. In this manner, a practitioner can assess and treat the whole body health by placing acupuncture needles in the ear, or by activating pressure points in the subject's hand or feet. In a similar manner, consider how DNA (the whole pattern or essence of a person) is replicated in each cell. And thus, while holding "only a dead" strand of the person's hair, we nevertheless have in our hands the complete pattern of their most intimate reality—their genetic DNA code.

Handwriting analysis can give most of the salient features of a personality with "just" one signature or a one sentence sample of handwriting. In so many aspects of our lives—from physical to mental to emotional to psychic— we carry our complete reality translated into every little part of us. Forensic science can work with very small parts indeed to locate the complete person; from such tiny samples as a drop of blood, a bit of sweat, a little swab of saliva and a very old and tiny bone fragment. Once again, the whole is represented in each little part.

And so it is with a piece of wood; although it has been cut off or otherwise separated from the complete tree, or even if that tree no longer exists in physical form located in time and space…nevertheless the morphogenetic field of that tree operates with that wood piece as a portal. This piece of wood can and does transmit to an open receiver, us, the essence of that tree type, the metaphysical characteristics of the tree and the healing energies available for those who are willing to be a recipient.

Wood is not plastic, but is a living thing in a different form from when it was recently part of the tree. That wood wand or pendant or spoon was not factory made but grew with its roots down into Mother Earth. And it survived for dozens of years or centuries—had a myriad of experiences including spiritual realities—and nevertheless continues to freely give of its essence, the power of the complete tree and the spiritual offerings of that particular tree.

People intuitively treasure keepsakes, of those who have died, for a reason, such as grandpa's flannel shirt, mother's wedding ring, their little child's cradle or a faded photograph of an aunt. Objects offer more than visual information. Touch and you will know, open your heart to information that arrives from all your senses. Your wood object will connect you to the spirit of the tree, and you can listen and communicate back and forth. Mind is not limited to body or a particular physical space but Universal Mind connects us all. And to be honest, Spirit transcends words and meanings…yet it is worthwhile to be so moved to love all of creation, to appreciate the essence, the spiritual power of trees. We have only to respect the trees and they will freely give to us.

Tree Spirit or Nature Spirit (Which Ministers to the Tree)?

There are a myriad of creatures which inhabit our universe and those who are curious about folklore, mythology or simply good science fiction, will freely discuss the wide range of human and non-human intelligences that could be "out there". One has to question why there are so many stories from the olden times about the fairy folk, also known as nature spirits. And what is the delineation between spirits found around trees versus the spirit of the tree itself?

Searching for an answer, it is not readily clarified when one locates the definition of a tree spirit as a "supernatural being <u>associated</u> with a tree". Now I am not saying that we should worship trees or anyone but the Great Creator but it is intriguing that every old or even ancient culture had names and stories for tree spirits. From Japan, there are a group of names but we can pick one, *kodama*. From Greece we have the tree *nymphs*, in India there are the *yakshis* and in Lithuania there were the *laumes*.

Many cultures claim their native tree as the Tree of Life, and so-called cults of leaving offerings to the spirit of the tree, or tree spirits, fill the historical record. Sir James George Frazer, in *The Golden Bough*, reports "At Grbalj in Dalmatia it is said that among great beeches, oaks, and other trees there are some that are endowed with shades or souls, and whoever fells one of them must die on the spot, or at least live an invalid for the rest of his days." There were sacred groves that witnessed sometimes mortal sacrifices and where some were forbidden to enter. I question whether a tree itself wished to have one mortal kill another to lay at the base of its trunk as an offering. This seems to be, looking back over the centuries, as a barbaric way to compensate for an ambient guilt of cutting down other trees in the forest.

In the past, some tribes such as the Dieri of Australia believed that the spirits of their own dead take up residence in a particular grove of trees. In other cultures and countries it was commonly accepted that the ghosts of those who died of disease, out along the roadways or women in childbirth were located in certain trees. Amongst these natives and in communities across the world, offerings were made to propitiate the sensitive spirits and to avoid at all costs felling those trees. Some native beliefs encompassed the notion that the spirits residence in the tree could be either forced out by the death of the tree, or otherwise roam at will. These tree spirits were seen as mischievous at best or to the extreme of being feared as dangerous demons.

In human evolution, perhaps we can now graduate to a wise attitude that does not project our fears upon trees but sees the trees, and the tree spirits, as worthy of respect and attempts to understand them; both in terms of science and also in the arena of spiritual truths.

Pink Ivory carved bead art and photo by Thomas Freese

Index of Wood Attributes

To utilize this index, look through the alphabetical list of attributes or issues, and then note the wood two letter abbreviation to go to in the section with the Guide to the Meanings of Woods. As it may be helpful, following this index, below is the alphabetical listing of all the included woods with their two letter abbreviation.

Burdens (release of) AB, BB
Calming, Release Stress BC, CH, CM, HA, HE, HO, JO, LA, MO, OK, PA, PH, SW, SG, SI, WW, YT
Camouflage AP
Cancer Patients (could be of assistance) LP
Celestial Beings (connect to) ZW
Cellular and Tissue Healing SW
Cellular Strength MS
Changes (keeping in balance) MO, MS, GE
Childhood Trauma (healing and release) BL, HO, PH
Clarity and Purity of Thought AS, HY, LP, MO, MB, PM, TW
Cleanse Energy CT, HO, HY, OO, TK
Comfort KW
Compassion MS, TB
Confidence BN, PP
Connection with the Ancient Ones GE
Connective Tissues (Healing) ME
Cooking, Food Service (channeling love through) BO
Creative Inspiration through Silence and Truth YH
Creativity AK, AR, BL, BB, HY, LA, TW, WG
Crown Chakra AS, BM, BC, JO, OL, SY
Courage BA, CV
Curiosity (promoting) RB, YT
Curses (breaking of) TH, GE
Depression/Sadness/Loneliness (Gives Comfort) BM, CY, PK, TB
Determination MT
Detoxing Parasites from the Body RB
Detoxing Physical and Emotional DG
Discernment in Healing Work BI, BX
Discernment in Life Direction BL, EU
Discernment with People BE
Divination LC, LV
Divining Rods HO
DNA codes (raising of) CW

Dowsing AD, RN
Ear Chakras (good for) JO
Earth Changes (warns of) BI
Earth Grids (connecting to) PMR
Earth Star Chakra PH
Earth Wisdom, Mineral Kingdom ZW
Elementals (controlling) AD, GE
Emotional Flexibility ME
Empath Remaining Aware and Objective LA, MS
Empathic Overload (preventing) BM, MA
Encouragement TB
Endurance against the Elements PI
Enemies (awareness of) RD
Energetic and Metabolic Balance (restoring) DG
Etheric Cords to Past and Others (cutting) MK, MB
Evil Spirits (warding off) WG
Exorcism Rituals PN, RM
Eyes (improving) BE, BB, EU, MG, MQ, YH
Faith in Spirit HY
Faithful Friendship or Love IV, MO
Fairy Energy BN, HY, OK, PR, PMR, SI, BW
Fear, Hate and Jealousy (understanding) MG
Fears (overcoming) MG, MA, PI, YH
Feelings (opening up) EU
Feet Chakras BC
Female Health HC
Fertility in Goals, or Birth AR, HC, SC
Fishing (good luck in) HW
Flexibility, Softness BE
Focus on Present Moment CH, HC, KW, PR, PMR, RH, TW
Forgiveness JO, PT
Friendly, Help the Underdog BW
Generosity of Spirit HR, PM
Glands and Body and Metabolism (enhancing) WW
Goals (attainment of) CT, DG, EU, TW

Good Boundaries/Support Others without Being Drained
BL, MK, MS
Good Decision Making AR
Happiness and Sunshine SQ
Harmony and Connection with Nature OL, PH
Healers Move and Rearrange Energy BI, MK
Healing (general) AJ, AW, BI, BU, BY, BX, CW,CY, DG,
ER, FL, HE, IP, IV, LV, MQ, NT, NR, OK, PC, PMA,
PMR, PN, PM, RN, SD, SG, SY, TH, TB
Healing of Burns BR
Healing (Physical) AJ, BY, BM, CW, CT, LV, PN, PM,
SG, SW, SY, WW
Healing (Physical) Wounds AD
Healing Through Absorbing Energies BX
Healthy Cell Growth CW, LP
Heart (physical health) CW, PT
Heart Chakra AB, AP, AS, BO, CW, HE, HO, LN, MB,
OO, PA, PMA, RB, SY
Heartbreak (healing) PMA
Heart Energy Balance CW
Heavy Energy Transmuting to Lighter Energy AB, BB
Help Others Find Their Way MG
Higher Self (aligning with) LA
Honesty HA, MY
Humor and Laughter as Best Medicine BW
Hyperactivity (Balancing Out) JO
Ideas and Concepts (discovering new) MG
Ideas to Fruition HC
Immunity MS
Independence and Completing Things WG
Inflammation (reducing) CW
Inner Strength AB, HC, LA, ZW
Inner Truth GE
Insights, Imagination, Intuition YH
Inspiration BB, HZ
Instant Energy AP, TW

Intelligence HZ
Intentions (focusing of) OK
Intestinal Area (physical healing) HE
Intoxication (preventing) IV
Intuition and Self-trust LA
Jealous and Envious People (repelling) AR
Journey in Meditation SF, YT
Joy, Harmony, Childlike Purity KW, MO, PM, RH, RB, RM, TW, WG, YH, YT
Joyfulness, Peace BB, CE, GV, PT, PM, RB, TW, WG
Kidneys and Adrenal Issues CV
Kindness to Others PM, PP
Knees (helping) SF
Knowledge RD
Kundalini Energy (Strengthen Balance of) HC, PMR, ZW
Leader CV
Life's Purpose MA
Light Within our Hearts (awakening) MG
Lightning Strike (protect against) ER, HZ, RN
Like Minded People Bringing Together PA
Liver Detoxification SW
Longevity CY
Longevity in Relationships SW
Love AP, AS, EM, FG, GS, HR, IV, JO, LI, MS, PMA, RO, YH
Luck and Success BU, IP, LC
Lungs (Helpful) LN
Magic of Dreaming MO
Maintain Efforts BS
Male Potency HW
Manifesting with Joy DG, EU, MO
Meditation (good for) AS, BE, BI, BU, LA, YT
Memory (Helpful) LN, PI, SY
Mental Clarity and Physical Health JO
Messages from Angels, Ascended Masters, Spirit Guides BL, HE, PR

Metabolism and Glandular Functioning DG
Missing People (finding) BI
Motivation and Staying Focused PMA
Motivator BE, BB, PMA
Moving energy TB
Multi-dimensional Visitors AP
Native American Spirits CE, MQ, BW
Needs of Others (providing for) LA, MG
Negative Perception Transmuted into Wonder and Awe YT
Negativity (Cleansing from Home) BM, CT, GE, HW, GE
Negativity from Others (repelling) BS, CH, GE, ER, LP,
ME, MA, MK, PK, PN, GE
Negativity (release of) WG, YT, GE
Nerve and Genetic Disorders (Healing) SG
New Information and Ideas BM
Nurturing energy TB
Old Emotional Wounds and Karmic Ties from Past
(healing of) OO, PMA
Opening to Possibilities BO
Palm/Hand Chakra BI
Pain/Discomfort (relief of) BX, TW
Pain (release of: Emotional, Physical, Mental and Sexual)
TW
Passions (Balance and Moderate) BN
Past Experiences (learning from) MO, MB PA
Past Lives (seeing) TW
Peaceful Sleep LI, MG, RM
Peacefulness KW, PM
Pent up energy (release of) BN, HO
Perseverance, Determination CE, CV, ME
Personal Growth (speeding path to) PR, SF
Personal Truth RH
Physical Love Passion NT
Pineal Gland (clearing out) BM, SI
Playfulness and Optimism OK
Pride (boosting positive) OO

Portal to Fairy Realm (opening) HR, PR, PMR
Portals to Other Realms (Guarding) ER
Positivity BX, HW, LC, LP, LV, PP, RH
Power of the Ocean AK, IK
Powerful Tool GE, NR
Procrastination (preventing) SW Prosperity BR, HY
Protection (Against Malevolent Forces) BK, BP, GE, ER,
KO, NT, WG, GE, ZC
Protection (Home) BR, BK, WG, GE
Protection (Self) AJ, BY, BL, BK, CH, CY, FL, FR, GE,
HR, HY, IP, IV, MT, PK, RO, SF, SQ, TK, TH, WG, VM,
ZC
Psychic Energies in Face (clearing) PR
Psychic Powers (increasing) BY, BM, BC, HY, MA, PT,
RO, RM, RN
Psychic Protection AV, BM, BL, BK, NT, WG
Public Speaking, Communication, Singing PK, PM, PP
Purification BY, CT, FL, HY, HW
Rain (bringing) HR
Reflection and Gratitude HE
Reconnecting with Lost Aspects of Self PI
Receiving and Releasing Energy SQ
Relaxation and Freedom MO, MQ
Remembrance of People, Past Events RM
Romantic Love PC, RO, SC
Root Chakra and/or Grounding to Physical Reality BM,
CE, CH, CV, EU, GE, HO, KX, LN, MG, ME, MK, MQ,
OL, PA, PH, YT, ZW
Stress and Fear (removal of) AR, MG
Sacral Chakra AR, BE, BB, HA, HC, HO, MA, PT, PM,
YT
Self-empowerment BC, HY, MS
Self without Judgement CH, MQ
Self-worth PT, TB
Serenity, Quietude BX
Sexual Attraction ER

Shamanic Spirit Teachers (connecting with) YT
Shapeshifting Magic PN
Shock, Upheaval (recovering from) PMR
Situations (leaving behind difficult) ME
Solar Plexus LP, MK,OO, TW, WG
Soles of Feet Chakras PMR, ZW
Soothing AS, BI, HE
Sore spots on body (release of) BN
Soul Ugliness Release and Replace with Love for All OL
Speaking up MG, OK
Spirit Guides (connecting with) AS
Spiritual Growth LP
Stability (Emotional, Mental and Physical) EU, GE
Stagnant Energy (moving out) PR
Strength from Mother Earth AW, BM, HA, LP, PMR, PH, SW, ZW
Strength in Self AK, AS, BA, BP, BY, BC, BX, CN, HC, LA, MK, MS, MT, ZW
Strength of Goodness LV
Suppressed Emotions (release of) PR
Third eye Chakra BC, BB, CM, GE, HY, JO, KW, LA, LN, MO, MG, PT, SY, TW, YT
Thoughts (simplify and focus) JO
Thymus and General Well-being WW
Toxic Relationships (release from) BL
Toxins (discharging from the body) BM
Tragedy (dealing with) BI
Trance States DG
Transformation GV
Travel, Loves People BE
Traveling TW
Throat Chakra BS, BE, OK, PK, SY, TB
True Identity (clarifying) MO
Trust in Being Supported and Grounded LN
Truth and Secrets BS, HA, PT, SF
Understanding AS

Universal Connection and Enlightenment BM, HY, PI, SI
Unwanted Energies (cleansing of) WG
Upper Heart Chakra BO
Violent Assault (protect against) HR
Vision, Daydream and Connect with Possibilities for Self
SF, YH
Vision Issues (Corrects Minor) MG
Voice of Ego (turning off) AS
Voice of Ego balancing with Inner Knowing SY
White Light Waves HY
Wisdom of Ancestors MQ
Wishes Come True HZ
Witchery (protecting against) RN
Yin Yang (balancing of male and female energies) PR

Alphabetical list of woods with their two letter
abbreviations:

Acacia Koa (AK)
African Blackwood (AB)
Alder (AD)
Alligator Juniper (AJ)
Apple (AP)
Apricot (AR)
Ash (AS)
Australian Blackwood (AW)
Avodire (AV)
Basswood (BS)
Bay (BY)
Beech (BE)
Birch (BI)
Blackberry Bramble (BR)
Black Laurel (BA)
Black Limba (BM)
Black Locust (BL)
Black Poisonwood (BP)

Blackthorn (BK)
Bloodwood (BO)
Bocote (BC)
Boxwood (BX)
Bubinga (BB)
Buckeye (BU)
Butternut (BN)
Camellia (CA)
Canary wood (CW)
Cedar (CE)
Chakte Viga (CV)
Chechen (CN)
Cherry (CH)
Chestnut (CT)
Clematis (CT)
Cottonwood root (CW)
Crepe Myrtle (CM)
Cypress (CY)
Dogwood (DG)
Ebony/Gaboon Ebony (GE)
Elder (ER)
Elm (EM)
Eucalyptus (EU)
Fennel (FL)
Fig (FG)
Fir (FR)
Gorse (GS)
Grapevine (GV)
Hackberry (HA)
Hawthorn (HW)
Hazel (HZ)
Heather (HR)
Hemlock (HE)
Hickory (HC)
Holly (HO)

Honeysuckle (HY)
Ipe (IP)
Iroko (IK)
Ivy (IV)
Jobillo (JO)
Katalox (KX)
Kingwood (KW)
Kou (KO)
Lacewood (LC)
Larch (Tamarack) (LA)
Laurel Negro (LN)
Leopard Wood (LP)
Lignum Vitae (LV)
Linden (LI)
Macassar Ebony (ME)
Magnolia (MO)
Mahogany (MG)
Makore (MK)
Maple (MA)
Mesquite (MQ)
Mimosa (MS)
Monterillo (MT)
Mulberry (MB)
Myrtle (MY)
Narra (NR)
Nettles (NT)
Oak (OK)
Olive (OL)
Osage orange (OO)
Paduak (PK)
Paperbark Tree (PT)
Pau Rosa (PA)
Pear (PR)
Persimmon, American (PM)
Persimmon, Asian (PMA)

(Asian) Persimmon Root (PMR)
Pine (PN)
Pink Ivory (PI)
Plum (PM)
Poculi (PC)
Poplar (PP)
Purpleheart (PH)
Redbud (RB)
Redheart (Chakte Coc) (RH)
Rhododendron (RD)
Rose (RO)
Rosemary (RM)
Rosewood (RW)
Rowan (RN)
Sassafras (SF)
Sea Grape (SG)
Sequoia (Redwood) (SQ)
Shedua (SD)
Snakewood (SW)
Sweet Chestnut (SC)
Suriname Ironwood (SI)
Sycamore (SY)
Tambootie (TB)
Teak (TK)
Thistle (TH)
Tiger Wood (TW)
Tulipwood (TW)
Vermelha (VM)
Black Walnut (BW)
Wenge (WG)
Willow (WW)
Yellowheart (YH)
Yew (YT)
Zebrawood (ZW)
Ziricote (ZC)

Definitions of Metaphysical Terms

Chakras (general) Chakra is an East Indian Sanskrit word meaning wheel. There are seven main locations for the main chakras in the "subtle body" yet corresponding to a line from the base of the spine in the human body and progressing up to the top of the head. For those who readily perceive these energy centers, they are described as spinning and also at times as a vortex; that is, they are funneling from their subtle body location to funnel-like progressively larger circles out from the body.

Another historical descriptor used is "psycho-spiritual vortices" of prana or "life energy". While we can identify the physical human body as mass, the chakras would be labeled energy. In spiritual and holistic treatment, these two, physical body and subtle body, interact. The theory holds that mind affects emotions which manifests in health or disease in the physical body. Thus many healers locate imbalances in the subtle body energy points, or chakras, and work directly with those to rebalance and effect healing in the physical body. Each main chakra has a color and psycho-spiritual sphere of experiential reality as it intersects with mortal life (see below).

This very truncated definition and overview is both a simplification and skips over the additional dimensional energetic systems…but this will suffice for an adequate representation for the purposes of this book; that is how the spirits of trees work with the human energy systems, chakras, to offer us healing, rebalancing and ways to better our lives through their unique ministrations. In addition to the main seven chakras, spiritual sources identify chakras below the body itself, chakras in our hands and what is called "the upper heart" chakra centrally located above the level of the heart yet below the throat chakra. There is a 12 chakras system. Note: The subtle body could be further delineated into etheric, emotional, mental and spiritual bodies.

Root chakra is located at the base of the spine, and it also called the Muladhara. The color is red and this chakra connects to our being grounded, safe and secure.

Sacral chakra represents creative and sexual expression, and the color is orange. It is called Svadhisthana.

Solar plexus chakra is located near the navel and the color is yellow. It is called Manipura and it is the source of our personal power.

Heart chakra is located next to the heart along the subtle body's energy column. Its color is green and it is called Anahata. It is midway and is our connection between matter and spirit. It is associated with love and compassion, charity of others and psychic healing.

Throat chakra represents the ability to speak our highest truth, verbal expression. The color is blue and the name is Vishuddha.

Third eye chakra is the sixth chakra, located between the eyebrows. It is also called the third eye and gives us the ability to see within a sixth sense, that is, to perceive intuitively. The color is indigo and it is called Ajna.

Crown chakra is on the top of the head and is called Sahaswara. The color is violet, or purple, and this is the conduit of our spiritual connection with the Universe, or our higher self. It is the chakra of enlightenment.

Earth star chakra is reported to be from six inches, below our feet, to 36 inches below. Its purpose is to "coordinate the grounding cord that leads to one's body upward and downward to the center of the Earth". It has also been called "our magnetic imprint upon this place". It also represents our life path, our link to past lives and karma.

Hand chakras represent what are considered to be a grouping of small chakras in each hand, with the primary hand chakra in the center of each palm. Open hand chakras allow energy to flow into and out of the body, and are particularly important for healers (or for anyone else who works with their hands).

Reiki healing is a healing technique that, with training, allows a layperson or professional practitioner to channel universal positive and healing energies to another person, group, animal, dimensional creatures, mineral kingdom, plants or to one's self. Reiki training provides the education for levels of understanding, ethics, hands-on experience, symbols to be used and activation by a Reiki Master.

Flower of Life is a pattern of 13 circles that holds numerous symbolic meanings; it is one of many sacred geometrical constructions that is found throughout the world in art, architecture and sacred teachings.

Flower of Life, Art and Photo by Thomas Freese

Cellular memory is a model for the experience of organisms, including humans, in which experiences are encoded into the cell of the entire body as well as being processed in the nervous system and brain.

DNA Codes Our DNA holds energetic and emotional codes as well as the codes for physical appearance and health tendencies. DNA codes can be altered and rewritten to import results health, emotional stability, and bring joy.

Timelines are the layering of dimensions. They run in lineal fashion and do not usually intersect. The closer they align the less unexplainable turmoil we feel.

Karma refers to the soul meeting itself in terms of thoughts, words, actions or inactions that are made by a person. When good or bad comes back to meet the person who initiated those actions and those comeuppances happen within their lifetime—that is called cause and effect. However in the spiritual model of reincarnation, those effects which come due in succeeding lives are called karma.

Akashic Records the etheric remembrances of the lives of mortals, showing forth all the actions, thoughts, intents, emotions, words of each person has lived in the past. In the model of reincarnation, or transmigration, the Akashic records will provide the information of human as well as non-human lives, and also delineate where in the Universe those lives were played out; including spheres besides our planet.

Smudge (sage) is a Native American sacred object and ritual, taken up by many others. Desert sage, sometimes with added cedar, is made into a dried bundle and lit to burn a cleansing smoke. The smoke is wafted over people or objects and in homes to remove negativity, stagnant energies or to encourage some earthbound spirits to move away.

Elementals are the fairy folk, the Nature Spirits. Also called Devas and with additional names from mythology and metaphysical knowledge, the elementals support physical life while they exist and move between our 3-D dimension and the etheric realm. Four categories of elementals have their home in their respective elements; the element of undines is water, the element of sylphs is air, the element of earth is gnomes and salamanders are those creatures of fire.

Guides are helpers who exist in the spiritual dimension and who are available to help us, personally and collectively. Some people identify their guides by name and are keen to describe what kind of guide works with them, and even noting their name and historical provenance. The term guides can mean, variously for different folks: angels, ascended masters, animal spirits, fairy folk, interdimensional beings or space beings, particular saints or wise ones...and so on.

Earth changes describe both the natural and cyclical geologic processes for our planet, as well as referring to the predictions and possible playing out of major land shifts, such as earthquakes, pole shifts, climatic changes and disappearance of some known cities and civilizations while those lost to time rise again. Edgar Cayce, the sleeping prophet of Hopkinsville, Kentucky, gave a number of warnings and predicted earth changes.

Ascension considered by some to be the ultimate goal of our spiritual journey, rising above material identity and ego consciousness in order to identify with universal awareness. This plan and process involves the mastery of compassion for all, embrace of a positive, balanced aspect of self-love and transcending the model of forgiveness to move from perception to direct knowing of the Divine.

Binding (and other) spells, white and black magic are forms of intentional work, which come through a variety of traditions, including the lineage of witches, pagan and other earth-based spiritual ways.

Author's note: some sources for the meanings of woods, the uses of wands, and the lore and energetic offerings of trees come from these above-mentioned ways. These ways are not my experience, but I have included references on wood meanings that outline the uses of wood related to spells. With some of these entries, I have lightly edited out a few references that I didn't feel comfortable transmitting; while I make no judgment on the use, efficacy or moral or spiritual practices of others. As I lack knowledge of the witch tradition of spells I can only offer what appear to be sound wisdom about the characteristics of the varying trees and woods, particularly for the general use of healing and protection.

Appreciating Trees with All Senses

There are rich counsels in the trees. Herbert P. Horne

It is true that we see trees, with our physical eyes, yet we also experience trees over our full range of physical and metaphysical sensorial input. While our eyes are fascinated with trees, their humble beginnings in a sapling, the magnificent glory of a mature tree—with broad trunk, branches reaching in all directions, we can let our other senses enjoy all the beauty that a tree has to offer. In addition, the wood of many trees exhibits fluorescent light which can be seen with the aid of an ultraviolet light (also known as a UV-A or black light). The color varies from yellow to green and also red, orange and pink.

The sounds of trees vary from the creepy creaking of branches to the slight rustling of leaves in a gentle summer breeze. Different types of trees, of course, have varying kinds of leaf shapes and so there are variations in sounds from the crinkly autumn rush of an oak tree to the hypnotic rustle of cottonwoods. Also, there are the shocking rifle-like retorts of icy limbs breaking and falling to the ground in a winter storm.

Touch…most of us have indeed reached out to feel tree bark and here, of course, there is a wide range, from smooth willow to rough locust bark. Touch can involve pain or pleasure or other distinct body feelings, and many a child has felt the sting of a willow whip. Pick up the bumpy fruit of the hedge apple tree, or brush up against the delicate birch tree leaves. To know trees, you have to use all your faculties of perception.

Scents come from so many tree types and in so many ways; tree flowers in all their heady glory, cedar and other strongly aromatic woods, sassafras root and bark, the vanilla smell of Ponderosa pine bark, musty maple leaves fallen in November, heady honeysuckle, stinky Tree of Heaven and the glorious crisp and clean fragrance of a Christmas fir or spruce brought indoors. There is the earthy scent of mimosa and the pungent Ginkgo fruit. All the fragrances of fruit trees not only flowering but the ripening fruit; these are some of the gifts of our companion trees.

And that leads us to taste and there are so many flavors of trees that give us fruits and nuts to enjoy. At a certain childhood age when I was growing up, I had only eaten canned peaches. When visiting a neighborhood friend, his mother offered me a fresh cut peach…and a whole new world opened up! I remember being out at my great aunt's farm when my older sister Jane showed me how to sample honeysuckle nectar by pulling out the string from a flower. Children play in trees and bushes, and they are immersed in all the senses of appreciating trees and shrubs. Also, some tree flowers that are reported to be edible include hibiscus, elderberry and apple. It's a good idea to research the topic online for cautions, including tree parts that cannot be safely eaten.

In addition to the five basic senses, we also are aware of temperature differences, and who has not, on a brutally hot summer day, headed straight for the cool shade of a grove of trees? One of my favorite walks, when I lived in Lexington, Kentucky, was to park and walk east to the pine grove at Masterson Station Park. There I wandered into the "back 40" where logs were set up as horse jumping obstacles. I lied down on the wide log and gazed up to the canopy of pine branches, with their healing green needles. I felt protected, nurtured and there was a magical quiet within that line of pine trees. These are the kinds of experiences that draw us to trees, that allow us to release the stresses of busy human life and that open our hearts and mind to the more subtle energies available in nature.

Which leads to yet another, non-physical sense and that is the mind communication that occurs between humans and trees. It could be termed telepathic, or intuitive, or instinctive or spiritual or interdimensional.

Photo from Pixabay tree-2127699_960_720

"Find tongues in trees, books in the running brooks, sermons in stones, and good in everything."
William Shakespeare, As You Like It

Grief for the Loss of a Tree

"Man is now becoming controller of the world forests and is beginning to realize how much these are needed by the planet. But he covers acres with one quick-growing species, selecting trees for economic reasons with no awareness at all of the planet's needs. This shows utter ignorance of the purpose of trees and their channeling of diverse forces. The world needs us on a large scale. Perhaps if man were in tune with the infinite, as we are, and were contributing his share, the forces would be in balance. But at present, the planet needs more than ever just what is being denied it— the very forces which come through large and stately trees." 8 May 1967 Monterrey Cypress Deva, channeled by Dorothy Maclean, page 99, The Findhorn Garden

When I lived in Lexington, Kentucky, I had one favorite tree that I loved to visit. It was an old legacy Ash tree on the former grounds of Ashland, Henry Clay's original estate. The tree was on a north facing angular short hill two thirds way down the green lawn on the property of a Shriner's Hospital. The pretty grounds that surrounded Shriners were sometimes visited by neighbors who appreciated the open space and a place to pay a brief visit, sometimes as they walked their dog. That north side hill, actually is still called Shriner's hill, and is a popular spot for families to go sledding when there is a good snowfall.

My friends, Don and Marilynn, who live not far from that place, introduced me to the "Shriner's walk" when I first visited Lexington, and later when I moved there and lived in Chevy Chase, I would often go there. I loved the openness, which reminded me of New Mexico.

And there were more than a few trees, both native and trees planted by Shriners. But that old ash tree, which likely was living back in the 1800s when Henry Clay had Ashland built for his daughter. It had the characteristics of a wise old tree, with twisted branches, huge main trunk, and showing the trauma of storms past. It shed the twirling double winged seeds in late spring. I think I recall a local hawk sometimes perched on bare branches in fall and winter.

One very long and busy day I drove to Cincinnati, through thunderstorms and traffic and the mess of construction on the widening of lanes for Interstate 75. I taught an art workshop at a convention and returned behind more traffic, jostling for lanes with big semi-trucks. The first thing I thought of to calm my nerves was to not head home but go directly to the green space of Shriners, to visit my favorite tree and soak up the steadying energies that a legacy tree can impart.

But when I pulled my car into the parking lot, I noticed that a fire engine was pulling away. A quick glance past the fire truck showed me that the old ash was down and smoking, having succumbed to the storm's lightning strike. In shock, I parked and walked from my car directly to the tree. In an instant, it had transformed from a proud elderly upright tree to a low lying mess of cut up logs and thrown down branches. There were two neighborhood kids there, on the bicycles, and one boy, excited by the fire truck and the adventure of this dramatic change remarked to me, "Isn't it cool!?" I just nodded his way, wondering if I could save something. I gathered a handful of seeds and, through the pungent smoke smell, just returned to my car and drove home. Something very powerful was lost for me.

We do have relationships with trees. They give us so much and ask for very little, just like friendships, they ask for respect and appreciation. When we lose a tree, we suffer that loss and grieve. You can stand on the tree stump, and if you are sensitive, you can still feel the energy of the tree that once occupied that space. Actually, a good part of the tree, the root system, is still there, below your feet. Once when I was traveling in Alaska, a friend drove me from Anchorage to Girdwood. We walked down a trail from the main lodge, and I put my hands on the trunk of a large cottonwood tree. I am a Reiki healer and I know the tingling feeling of healing energy as it moves through my hands. The feeling of my two hands at that moment could only be described as electric! It was so strong I had to bounce my hands off the trunk.

There are trees that I have known and lost. When I walked in my neighborhood in Santa Fe, New Mexico, I loved to walk past beautiful old poplar trees. I admired their brilliant yellow fall leaves contrasting with the perfect blue southwest sky. One day, I came around the corner to find the main old tree cut to a stump; evidently, there would be a widening of that street…a necessary expediency. But I was so upset that I marched home, got a small piece of plywood, sawed it into the rough shape of a gravestone, and painted, "RIP here lies our beloved poplar tree." I returned to put the marker against the stump, as drivers honked in appreciation of that spontaneous testimonial.

True Tales of Encounters with the Nature Spirits

The following are true tales of encounters with the spirits, the beings that live around trees. I think it's important, when considering tree spirits and wood energies, to know about those companion spirits who love and live intimately with the magnificent trees on our planet. The first story can be found in one of Ted Andrew's books, "Enchantment of the Faerie Realm"...

Ted Andrews:

There are others of the faerie realm who also gather and live around trees, in woods and forested areas. To the Greeks, they were known as dryads. To most people they are simply known as wood nymphs. They are still found in wooded and forested areas—especially those that are somewhat wild.

The wood nymphs are usually female, and wear little or no clothing. Glimpses usually show them as dancing in the sunlight that comes through trees. They sing beautifully, often imitating the birds. They understand the language of animals and humans. They have a great curiosity about humans, and although they usually avoid direct contact, they will risk it for the opportunity to observe humans.

Sometimes the wood nymphs will appear childlike, and they are drawn to certain kinds of trees. They are very playful and rejoice in all expressions of nature in their environment. In an area of the wood where I grew up that we called "Fort Apache" was a young wood nymph, although I did not realize it at the time. It was a young girl who always had a squirrel at her feet. I would see her occasionally spying on us through the trees while we played.

Once when I went to that area by myself, she came from behind the trees. She did not speak a lot, and she often laughed at my expressions, but never in a mean way. Her laugh was contagious, and she let me pet her squirrel. She had a knack for avoiding my questions. She would just laugh when I asked her why I never saw her at school. Her answer to my question as to where she lived was always the same: "Around here." When I asked her name, she would pretend she didn't hear. To this day, I still do not know what her name was. Whenever she seemed tired of my questions, she would erupt with wonderful laughter and then run in among the trees, disappearing.

I remember the last time I saw her. I had gone to that area alone again. I wasn't sure if I would see her or not, as her appearances were becoming more and more scarce. I found her sitting by the creek with her feet in the water. She was crying. The squirrel was not with her, which I found to be very curious. I stood there, feeling awkward and wishing that I hadn't come out looking for her.

She looked up and gave me a half smile as if she heard my thoughts. I asked her if she were alright, and she stood and said she was.

"Why are you crying?" I asked.

"I have to leave," she answered softly.

I remember shivering as the trees rustled with a sudden breeze. She stepped up to me and kissed me on the cheek. I was surprised. She laughed at my expression and then dashed off among the trees. I heard her call out, "I will remember you, Ted Andrews."

And then she was gone. I never saw her again. The next week, developers started clearing the area to build some new houses.

From pages 163-165 in Enchantment of the Faerie Realm:
Communicate with Nature Spirits & Elementals
by Ted Andrews © 2002 Llewellyn Worldwide, Ltd. 2143 Wooddale Drive, Woodbury, MN 55125. All rights reserved, used by permission.

Photo from Pixabay dryad-1392438_960_720

Dad Was a Water Witch

Sybil Watts

Farmer with dowsing wood Photo from Wikipedia (original copyright from England expired)

Author's note: I met Sybil years ago and she told me some stories about the amazing gift her father, J. W. Watts, utilized in order to help both his own family and others in their community. Sybil grew up on a farm in Muskogee County, in northeast Oklahoma.

There are skeptics of the process of dowsing, or water witching. Some studies in controlled conditions report results "no better than chance". Scientists refer to the ideomotor effect of our own muscles creating the tiny movements they say result in the directional pointing of the dowsing tools. In olden times, the church at times condemned the practice while other church authorities, after the dowser found abundant clean water for their monastery, called the results miraculous. I suppose each person will respectively have their own opinion to either debunk or affirm the energetic or spiritual nature said to be in effect.

I tend to believe that the spirit of the tree assists the water witch, and this collaborative effort and tool, when used respectfully for good, has positive results that accumulate anecdotal evidence.

I was nine years old in 1962. It was a bright summer day. I sat in my favorite perch, high up in the old Black Walnut tree in the backyard. The foliage was thick and the perch was comfortable enough to sit and read for hours, hidden from the demands of everyday life.

I looked up from my book to see dad out in the peach orchard. He was walking among the trees, pulling and examining a limb here, letting it go and moving to another. Finally, he found what he was looking for, pulled out his knife and cut off a branch. Then he started stripping it. Hmm?? This called for further investigation.

So I climbed down from my perch and took my curious self out to the orchard to watch and question. Dad was so busy preparing his branch; he did not hear me approach.

He was startled when turned around to find me standing there, all wide-eyed and curious.

"Whatcha doin'?"

"Getting a witchin' rod," he replied.

"A what? Whatcha gonna do with it? What is it for? Why do you n—"

"One question at a time. This is a Y rod. I use it to find water. I'm what is known as a Water Witch."

To me, it looked a lot like a chicken or turkey "wishbone."

"What's the straight one for?"

"I use it to mark the place for the diggers."

"Oh. Why did you get it from a peach tree?"

"Because peach trees are generally good at finding water in strange places."

"Why did it take you so long to find one?"

"The rod has to be the right thickness with a Y in just the right place to use it to find water. Too many details to explain right now."

"How does a peach limb find water?"

"Here, I'll show you. See, I happen to know where the steam runs that provides the water for our well. So let's start with that. You walk beside me so you can see what happens when I find the water."

"How do you know where our water comes from?"

"Because I witched that well long before I ever thought about you, before I even knew your mom. Ok. Now if you want to see this, you have to walk beside me and be quiet. No more questions until I say it is ok. OK?"

"OK."

So he stuck the straight stick in his hip pocket and turned the Y up so that he could hold one side in each hand and we walked down the garden away from the house and I didn't see that stick move at all. I had so many questions I wanted to ask. However, I knew if I started talking Daddy would just go and not finish this lesson. And I really wanted to know what he was doing with that weird stick. Anyway, I thought witches were supposed to be bad and my Daddy wasn't bad. I quietly marched along beside him, intently watching that stick do . . . nothing.

Suddenly, he stopped. "Do you see? The stick is staying still in my hand."

"Yeah, I see that. Did you find water?"

"No. That is how we know there is no water here. The sticks don't move."

"But I thought you were going to show me how to find water, 'cause you know where to look already?"

"First, you had to know how to know that you have not found water."

"Now, here we go." And he walked a little ways in a crosswise direction and suddenly that stick started to quiver. Then it began to pull downward. And suddenly THUMP! It went straight down. Dad looked at me. I was wide-eyed and slack jawed. "How did you do that?"

"I did not do that. The water flowing underground did that. When you find water, it pulls the top end down when you get right over water. Now watch."

He began walking back a different direction. Then he walked what he called "out of range" and the stick started to move back up. He turned around and walked back to where I stood and as he came nearer the stick started to quiver and once again, THUMPED down.

Then dad forced it straight out in front of him and said, "Watch. I'm asking it to show me the direction of the water flow." He began to turn around. The stick pulled back toward me. "See, I found the water and it is flowing in your direction. Where is the well?" Well, I knew the answer to that. Without even looking I pointed in the direction of the well.

"Right. So when I'm out on a job looking for water, I follow the direction of the flow to see if it will go to where the client wants to dig his well." He turned in the direction of our well and walked toward it. The Y-rod pointed down and forward while he walked. When he got to our well, he veered off in a different direction. The stick pulled back to the well. No matter which way he turned, the rod pulled back to the well. Except when he turned in the direction of the flow, then the rod would stay out in front of him.

Then he told me how deep the well is and how much water would flow through it. I asked "How do you know that? That well was already there when we moved here."

He said, "I told you, I witched it. A long time ago."

"Have you ever witched wells since I was born?"

"Yes. Often."

"How come I never seen you cut a limb off our peach tree before?"

"Because usually, I know the area I'm going to and I know that there are probably trees there that are better for the purpose. The local trees know where the water is and makes my job much easier. I prefer Willow. Peach is second best. Today, I don't know the area, and looking on the map, does not look like there is a reliable source of water, so I'm not sure what kind of trees are there. So I'll take this one with me, just to be prepared."

"So how do you know all that about the size and everything?"

"I don't really know how I know. I just do. I feel it by how the stick pulls. I know how much water is flowing. How deep to dig. How much water the well will provide. And I can tell what it tastes like."

"Do you always find water?"

"No. Sometimes there is no water in the area where people think they want to dig a well or a pond. Usually, I can find some water in the area, but it is not always enough to warrant digging."

"Did anyone ever dig a well and not get water?"

"You mean did someone dig a well that I witched and not get water? Not if they listened to me. A couple times the farmer thought he knew best and dug a well where he wanted to dig it, and didn't get water. But I told him there was no water there."

"Do you charge people for going and finding them water?"

"No it is a gift and if I charge for it, I will lose the gift. OK. Enough questions. I have to go." The lesson was over.

Over the years, until his death, he was called on by people from miles away to locate wells. He could tell how deep to dig, how big the hole needed to be, how much water the well would provide and what it would taste like.

Shortly after the incident in the garden, Dad bought a farm really cheap. 40 acres for nearly nothing. Because the owners thought it was dry and there was no water. Dad went out and walked before purchase. He KNEW exactly where the water was. In the 7th year of what turned out to be a 10 year drought in Oklahoma, he had a pond and a well dug on that property. People who did not know dad very well thought he was crazy.

When the dozer was working on the pond, dad wanted the pond to be approximately 20 feet deep and a pretty large circumference. He stood out there watching as the man worked, digging out the area for the pond. Finally, dad had him to stop and pointed out a big rock in the middle of the area. He told the guy, "Be careful. Don't dig up that rock until you are finished. I want the pond deeper and bigger and I don't want your dozer to get stuck in here." The guy was like, "Yeah, whatever." He did not believe dad, as he did not know his reputation.

When the dozer pulled up that rock, water shot 100 feet in the air! He barely got the dozer out. In a couple days, there was over 7 feet of water in the pond – during a time when there had been no rain for many months. The water was always very cold and it never went dry. People attempted to dive to where the spring was, but the power of the water was so strong no one could ever get all the way down to it.

Then when we were ready to move out to the farm, dad had a well dug near where he planned to put a house and plant a garden. That water was cold and sweet and delicious. And although we watered the garden and played in it, we never pumped that well dry. We sold the farm and the buyers built a big new house and used that well to modernize the house. The last I knew, the well was still providing all the water the family needed and the pond never went dry.

Did anyone ever dig a bad well that Dad witched? Yes. Dad's brother wanted a well on his farm so he could stop hauling water. Dad located two sources of water. The one near the house was Sulphur. Dad told Uncle although there would be lots of water, the water was Sulphur and not drinkable, don't dig there. However, the one farther away was clear and would taste delicious and provide all the water the household would ever need. Uncle did not want to run pipe that far (1,000 to 1500 feet) so he dug the well near the house. OMG!! When that well came in the whole area smelled like rotten eggs for days!!! Uncle went ahead and piped it into the house anyway. They used it for laundry and such and still had to haul drinking water.

When Uncle's son grew up and decided to put a mobile home on the property, Uncle had him set the home near where Dad had located the 2nd well, as they had marked it with an iron rod. Long after dad had passed on, Uncle dug that second well. It turned out to be the sweetest tasting water ever. Delicious and refreshing. Once the new well was dug, Uncle went ahead and piped it to the homestead. The single well supplied water to both homes and the garden, and to the best of my knowledge, still does.

Dad was vindicated.

This was Dad's way of locating water. Although I don't really know other dowsers, I'm sure there are others today with similar skills and their way of finding water is much different than what my Dad used.

No. I don't know whether I really have the gift of finding water. That was never anything I had reason to spend time in learning. I do us a pendulum and L-rods on a regular basis. My younger brother can locate water. I don't know whether he can provide details as Dad did.

Author's note: there are many references to the spiritual properties of peach.
The peach tree is traced back 7,000 years to China and Tibet, and carries wonderful beliefs and mythology in China. In addition books reporting the use of peach for varying rituals includes so-called folklore in some of the United States; including Kentucky, Missouri and Arkansas. The peach tree is said to symbolize immortality, protection and luck. In China, the carved peach pits were used as amulets and were said to bring fertility and magical powers.

The Angel and the Wand

By Rick Hayes

Friendships are formed as an essential element of the life circle, a bond of smiles and exchanging of thoughts and experiences.

I met Thomas several years ago at an industry event where he and I were one of the several featured speakers. As a Psychic Medium, often the opportunity to meet others in the field can be quite time restrictive due to public requests and scheduling during these events. When a few minutes of opportunity to say hello occurs, Thomas and I will take the benefit given to 'catch up' with smiles, laughter, and an exchange of what has been happening in our lives.

The evening before the doors open for an event is a time for setup along with a quick exchange of hellos amongst friends. While focusing on the stand up banners to make sure they were 'correctly sighted', I heard the familiar voice of a good friend. There stood Thomas, with a smile that emanates energy of instant happiness. It had been a year since last we met, and still expresses an infectious passion for his craft.

One of the crafts was his ability to create a mystical art form from wood. His ability to sense the mystical energy within a small branch from a tree was fascinating, and he happened to have an array of these one-of-a-kind wood wands on display at the show. With his smile, Thomas stated "stop by my booth when you get a chance this weekend Rick and take a look-see at these wands I have created. I would love to hear of any energy that you pick up from them".

Before the set-up evening was complete, I stopped by my friend's booth. Thomas unraveled a roll of protective cloth that covered some 50 plus wood energy wands. I could instantly see that each had its own unique feature created by this artist friend of mine. As he shared the type of wood that one was created from, I felt a strong sense of energy from a smaller dark rose colored energy wand. As I picked it up, the vibration was extraordinary. Before I left I stated to Thomas "Watch to see how many are drawn to this particular wand, begin to pick it up then will not." Thomas informed me that this scrolled wand was made from the Bubinga wood. Later when he shared with me what energy is defined from this wood, it made perfect sense. I also placed an offer to purchase if not sold through the weekend.

As the weekend wound down to a close, I stopped by to hear the outcome of how many were drawn to the Bubinga wand, and to inspect if the energy wand was still on display. Sure enough, the scrolled wand was there waiting for me. With the purchase and a hug of friendship, Thomas asked a favor. "If you have any experiences from the energy of this wand, let me know."

Ricky Hayes with his wand, photo by Thomas Freese

For some reason, I felt he would be hearing from me soon.

Upon arrival at home, it took me a couple of days to open my event luggage and take the Bubinga wand from its

137

pouch. I had a good reason – within a few days, I would be repacking for yet another speaking appearance. Upon removal, I placed the beautifully crafted wood on a plaster pedestal décor in my home office. Other items on the pedestal included a valuable angel statue and stone energies given to me by client friends. The wand was safe and secure on the pedestal without any opportunity of rolling off from its position. That is until the next day.

My day was complete, filled with scheduled psychic medium connections (readings) and inspiration. The day had turned to dusk as I sat at my desk in my home office reviewing the emails from that day. All was serene, until suddenly a thump interrupted the tranquility. Hearing those and seeing those in spirit is a part of my day and life, so for a few moments I simply relayed a 'thank you for your acknowledgment' and continued reviewing the emails on my laptop. After several seconds had passed, I turned my chair to see the Bubinga wand on the floor several feet away from the pedestal.

Now granted my 'normal' life includes visits with those in the next part of life continual, so items being moved are nothing new for me. In this case, I could not acknowledge a loved one in spirit. What I could acknowledge was the vibration from the small piece of wood on the carpeted floor.

A few days later Thomas and I met at yet another speaking event. I could not wait to share my experience, and the information he shared with me created an understanding.

He shared after research that the Bubinga wood is said to possess a giggling happy energy providing clarity and a sense of peace. It is an angelic realm (remember the angel statue on my pedestal?) that calms the stress.

My energy wand from a friendship is placed back in its position next to the angel statue. Just as the friendship, the wand will remain.

BElieve

For more information about Psychic Medium Rick Hayes, visit www.lifesgift.com

The Cloven Hoof Creature

Lydia Borin, Tampa, Florida

I take my dog Max for a walk every evening around my neighborhood. As the seasons change, I have to adjust which time of day for walks so Max does not overheat, pant too much, and I don't get too much sun. That means the walks have to be right after the sun is going down but before it gets dark.

About a year ago, (2001), I had to wait later and later for the walks because of the heat. This resulted in the last part of the walk being a little after dusk. We take the same path every day and I enjoy looking at all the flowers, plants and trees along the way. We also say hello to all the other people and their doggy owners taking walks.

There is one big tree down at the end of one road where we turn and walk around the loop. This tree has big trunks, some of which you could climb up on and sit. I often thought about when I was a kid and climbed up on the big branches of the willow tree in my yard in New Mexico to get away from my Mom and the willow switches she was chasing me with for misbehaving. The problem was, soon as I came down from the tree, she would be right back under the tree and get me. Ah, those special memories.

I got sidetracked so let me get back to the story. Each time Max and I walked by the tree, Max wanted to sniff the big hoof prints below the tree. These hoof prints were smunched into the ground as if something very heavy stepped all over. There is a fence around our community and no one has horses or big dogs so what made the hoof prints? Every evening I anticipated looking at the ground around the tree to see if new hoof prints had been made.

I seemed to be drawn to that tree every time we walked near the location. I have never really noticed it until looking at it with the sundown at dusk and seeing the hoof prints. There almost seemed to be a glow in one area of the tree where the tree limbs came together at the trunk.

As time went on, the glow seemed to get stronger and I began to see a little bit of a shape within it. One day as I looked up at the tree, I was stunned to see what looked like a creature standing within the glow. It was all hairy and the bottom part looked like haunches of a goat type creature with cloven hoofs. The head portion was hairy but had a very human aspect to it. It had a cape hanging around from the back of it. It shook me up but for some reason, it was not scary. I stood there and stared at it in awe. It looked out like a specter, ghost or fantasy creature and did not look completely solid. Then it seemed to disappear.

Now I could not wait until I went on our walks to see the Cloven Hoofed Creature. Each time the glow was there and then the creature would begin to materialize and stay there for a while only to disappear again. I began to feel the Cloven Hoofed Creature was a part of my life, something magic and unbelievable. After about a year, the Creature began to have a sort of saddened look on its face and the glow seemed to be getting dimmer.

One evening, the creature extended out its' arms, as if trying to tell me something. It then wrapped itself in the cape and began to disappear. Within the next few days, the image was less distinctive and one day it had just disappeared. The hoof prints were gone and I felt so very sad that this mysterious creature no longer seemed to exist.

I thought and thought about what could have happened. I thought about the Peter Pan story in which the children no longer believed in story creatures and this caused them to disappear until the children believed in them again. Well, I believed so that was not the problem. I decided to search the Internet for an answer. I checked several websites.

I had never checked such things as ghosts, specters and spirits, but that is exactly what I did. I found out a strange fact. It seems in different parts of the world where cell phone towers have been put up near known haunts and where mysterious sounds and creatures appeared routinely, they had slowly disappeared. Could this be what happened to the Cloven Hoofed Creature? Could the signals coming from cell phones affect whatever these beings are? I checked around our area and sure enough, one of those big towers for cell phones had been recently installed outside our neighborhood but within the vicinity of the creature's tree.

I was sorry my mysterious creature no longer seemed to exist. It was sad to walk by the tree and not see any hoof prints on the ground. Then just a month ago, I began to see a little glow in the tree again, just a tiny spark. I was so excited and each day I hurried on our walk with enthusiasm. Eventually, there were hoof prints again for

Max to smell. The Cloven Hoofed Creature was back, with a bright glow.

This made me wonder about the cell tower and phone conclusion. The next time I drove out of my neighborhood, I checked the cell tower and found it had been removed and set up further down the road. Could this be the reason the Cloven Hoofed Creature was back?

For now, I am just happy there is something glowing in the trees and smiling down at me. We are affected by our surroundings including our environment. Each time we look at the physical beauty of the world, a flower, sunset, wildlife and ponder the mysteries of life, my bead and fiber work evolves and begins new paths. When you are out walking where ever you live, look at your surroundings, soak it in, and be happy we are part of such a big world with many natural wonders.

Tree Spirit—Black Figure with Branches

Jane Freese, Santa Fe, New Mexico

On a summer evening two years ago, (2010), after a long day at work I spontaneously stopped by a friend's house in my old neighborhood from where I had recently and painfully moved. We had a delightful visit, snacked and talked—then as it was approaching evening—I left. I had moved further out past the area and down a long pot-holed winding road toward the railroad tracks. On either side of the road was a diverse selection of homes, from grey concrete block encampments, yurts in yards, funky faux adobes and to well-appointed beautifully designed homes. I had been living in my new place just a few months, post-divorce. Though it was a bit rugged, the area was beautiful and I loved the special feeling of the nearby preserve that I hiked many times over the last 20 years, for it seemed to have the most magical presence.

It was getting darker as I followed the road down past the cattle guard, breathing in the New Mexico summer evening air with the car windows open. Right before the sharp curve in the road—the place where you must respect your speed, as the arroyos on either side could claim your vehicle, my headlights flashed on a dark figure that dashed in an instant across the road—I gripped the wheel and slammed on the brakes! What flashed before me in a second looked like a black stick figure covered in black shreds of rags or roots or branches hanging from a bone thin stick like frame. Was it a tree with black branches? A person in rags? Whatever it was, it was running FAST, with leaps or almost skips....

My heart was beating and I was completely unnerved! I rounded two more narrow curves, passed the Galisteo Creek and railroad tracks, then around another sharp curve, and drove through the gate before I was home in the now complete dark.

I just couldn't get it out of my mind…I lay in bed wondering what sort of encounter I just had. Every time I drove past that same spot I simultaneously hoped and feared that I might see it again.

A few weeks later, we had torrential rains two days in a row—rare in the high desert—and the arroyo overflowed at that very spot. It is a mystery without any rational clue, and while it is branded in my psyche as without explanation, I have no doubt that it did occur.

Man of the Woods

Ruben Moreno, Louisville

One experience of interest came from a walk I took in Cherokee Park in Louisville, Kentucky in the mid-1990s. I remember there was no color, it was way beyond fall, the dead of winter. As I walked through the woods it was stick and bare branches. I went along the walking and bike path through the park. I was headed up the hill to Hogan's Fountain. After I had passed the little retreat area where the basketball court and fountain are, I went further into the park. The path forms a large "S" curve, going downhill. I had gone through the first half of the curve and I came to the wooded area, which is in front of the homes that line that area of the park. At that time I kept almost a running walk, keeping a pretty good pace. Being a walker, one doesn't want to stop because you'll lose the momentum, the burning of calories. So I have a tendency, whenever I see someone while walking, to give them a quick hand wave but to keep on going. That would keep me from getting into conversation.

As I came into the straightaway, I looked directly ahead to see a figure. He was in the thick brush, sort of rising upward. He had a sort of brown jacket that peeled off. The figure was totally unclothed. At first, I had a strange feeling as I looked at this person that he was looking directly at me and had a slight smile on his face. He had very curly hair. To say that he did or didn't have horns, I couldn't swear to it. But if he had horns they weren't large but rather thumb size.

146

I ignored him, thinking that it was just a winter's flasher. I continued on my brisk walk. As I came down into the "S" curve, I started mentally and emotionally processing exactly what it was that I did see. I began to realize that the man in the woods may not have been what I first thought he was. It dawned on me that it might not really have been a flasher but more of a Pan-type figure— someone from the forest world. His jacket was long. If he was a flasher, he would have popped it open, but in this case the man was taking off the jacket. I wondered if I saw someone going into transition from one form of reality into another. I've never experienced that ever again, in anytime or anyplace where I've lived in the country. And I've had woods of my own, went down into them frequently, and I've never that any other experience of that nature, whether flasher or Pan!

Author's note

After hearing Ruben's story I was curious to find out more about where in Cherokee Park this incident happened. So I looked up Hogan's Fountain and was surprised to find that the main figure of the fountain sculpture is none other than Pan himself!

Thomas Freese:

When I was given some persimmon wood, and before I had samples sent out to have my psychic friends tell me what they got on its meaning, I looked online but I didn't find anything about the spiritual meanings for persimmon in the usual sources. I continued to search with a wider net and found a posting by a lady who dreamt on the meaning of persimmon. She had heard Ozark folklore about persimmon, but her dream gave her, and us, a wonderful and important addition to the meanings for (American) persimmon. And here below is her story...

Wild Persimmons after the First Frost (Thursday, November 20, 2014)

Mickie Mueller

This summer, I discovered that we have a persimmon tree growing here at Aelfheim. I've never eaten a persimmon, so I was delighted. After reading up on wild Missouri persimmons I learned that they are bitter and astringent if not fully ripe. Yes, I did try, I was anxious and whew! I don't recommend it, better to wait. There is an old saying that persimmons aren't edible until after the first frost, so I waited. Sunday night we were hit with an early snow and freezing temperatures. We didn't get as much snow as my friends in the east—they can't get out their doors, but we got some snow. I woke up this morning having been dreaming about eating persimmons, and I remembered—it was time! I bundled up and headed out, the snow was melting and slippery as I made my way down to the persimmon tree.

Wow! A lot of creatures of the forest had gotten to them already. No doubt many had fallen to the ground and were under the snow. Most of them were too far up for me to reach, but I managed to gather seven of them. It's ok, it was mostly culinary curiosity and many of the wild birds rely on being able to forage for things like persimmons, elderberries and other wild plants, so I left most of them to the birds.

Now there is nothing beautiful about a wild Missouri persimmon. They are shriveled looking things. But I forged forth, cut one in half and examined the fruit inside. It was soft, gooey, sticky, doesn't really sound very good does it? I grabbed a spoon and managed to scoop the pulp away from the bitter skin and popped it into my mouth—bliss! Wow, really delicious! Its flavor was sweet and buttery like nature created the perfect candied fruit. If the sweetest plum nature could make had a baby with a really moist date whose uncle was a pumpkin...maybe it would taste like a persimmon. It's really not like anything I've ever eaten. Many people have seen Asian persimmons which are very pretty and look like little pumpkins, these aren't those persimmons. But don't judge a book by its cover. Ugly as it is to look at, the flavor is really a treat and there's something magical about picking something that grew in the wild and eating it!

I couldn't pick persimmons and eat them without examining their seeds for a weather prediction. There is a bit of folklore that says if you cut persimmon seeds in half you can find out what kind of winter you will have in your area. If the white inside the seed looks like a knife it means cold and ice. Spoon shaped means lots of snow, and a fork means a dry mild winter. So, the persimmon has magical properties, like most plants do. According to Ozarks folklore if you eat an unripe persimmon you will change your sex. Now I wouldn't take this literally, however it may be a bit of useful magic for someone going through a sex reassignment procedure to help you embrace the difficult changes with a little more ease, and even to use for magic to help others accept your true self. I personally would use a ripe persimmon though, the intention would still be there, and dears, unripe persimmons are just nasty. I love ya more than that! Other magical properties of the persimmon include healing, and good luck!

On the magic of persimmons, wait, there's more! In addition, I want to share a bit more information that the persimmon spoke to me of in my dream. As it reminded me that it was waiting for me in the field, ripe and lovely, I was told a story of its magical use. Its story was one of our status and station in life. How we accept our position and therefore agree to it. The persimmon's magic gives us an opportunity to help us rise above where we are, daring to dream of our own life beyond the other people's perception of us, stretching our abilities, and boosting our status in our work, community, and life in general. If you want to "level up" in the game of life, try looking beyond what you thought was possible, try working some magic with the persimmon. This is a little unassuming fruit that may not appear to be much upon initial inspection, but if we look deeper we discover something amazing in inner beauty that elevates it, delightful flavor, and even wisdom that lies within.

Fairy Lights

Leslie Moise

This happened on the last day of April, the eve of May Day in 2007. According to tradition, the winter and summer fairy courts change in May and October. The weather was cool, damp, clear—a little bit chilly. I was with a friend who has had fairy encounters too. We each had a holed stone. Naturally holed stones are supposed to facilitate seeing any fairies that are around. We had our holed stones for some time. We also were holding Merlinite which is a stone that helps one communicate with fairies and nature spirits.

We waited until twilight then we went to the deck behind my house. It used to be a hot tub deck, it's octagonal and I painted a labyrinth on it. It's seen a lot of meditation and spiritual activity. We went out, holding the Merlinite in one hand, the holed stones in the other hand. As we looked through the fairy stones we could see the aura of the trees. The area is not actually encircled by trees but it looks and feels like it is. As we looked at the trees we could see what might be similar to a 'heat shimmer'.

As we talked about what we saw, we moved in a clockwise circle on the deck. There is a large tree close to the deck that is quite tall. It has mistletoe on it so I have a number of names for this tree, such as mistletoe tree, or the monkey tree. It used to have a protrusion in the bark that looked exactly like a monkey's face. That was broken off during the ice storm of 2009. Sometimes we call it the 'yes' tree, because when you're walking toward it from a certain direction, the branches form a very definite "Y", the trunk shows an "E" and there is also an "S".

All of a sudden little tiny, white lights started streaking—not through the branches—but along the branches. There were hundreds of lights which increased until there were thousands. They were running all up and down the branches and the trunk, just in constant motion.

We both gasped and asked one another, "Do you see that?!"

"Yes, I do! Oh my gosh!"

We asked each other, "What do they look like?"

And together we both described little, white lights, moving so quickly. Sometimes my academic background steps in to try and find an explanation fitting in with science.

I asked, "Could those be fireflies?"

But as we looked through the holed stones I recalled that fireflies have a greenish tint. They waver and of course, they blink on and off. The lights we saw were not blinking, they moved in a totally different way, and they were definitely pure white. We jumped up and down with excitement and we stayed there and watched them for five or ten minutes.

My friend said, "Let's lower the holed stones and see if there are any other nature spirits or fairies that show up."

Then we lowered the holed stones to see the lights still there and when we returned the stones up to our eyes the fairy lights were still there. After about thirty minutes I think they were still present but the visual image faded away.

Since I've talked about this experience with others, one acquaintance told me she had a very parallel experience after the wind storm of September 2008 went through, the remnant of Hurricane Ike. She said she was sitting in her backyard at twilight, praying for the trees to heal after so many trees were damaged or destroyed, when she saw a very similar thing. She felt strongly that was the fairies helping to heal the trees.

Tree Spirit Friends

I was a tree climber as a child. I have nephews who go up in trees in order to hide from chores. But for me, trees were my friends. There was a little mulberry tree between our garage and our neighbor's garage. The trunk was angled in just the right way for me to lay there and nestle in the tree. And I would be up there for hours. There was a crabapple tree across the street in a neighbor's front yard. I loved that tree but I was <u>not supposed to climb that tree</u>.

The homeowner didn't like people being up in the tree because it would break the bark. I was a little tiny kid back then, a 'thread with a head', and I could climb up the tree so lightly. But I couldn't convey to the adults how I was being gentle with her. I would wait until after dark to climb up the crabapple tree. I felt a very comforting, sweet presence in that tree.

Later when I was in high school and starting college, my father was a professor of political science at the University of Louisville. We used to go see him on campus. There was a row of a half dozen crabapple trees near his office building. The tree blooms were a very rich cherry pink blossom and I recognized it as being a very similar color as the crabapple in my childhood. No matter what was going on, I would intentionally park in a place where to get to class I had to walk under those trees.

When they later were chopped down I was so very sad. I grieved because friends of mine had been killed.

155

Last year, I walked around the front part of my farm, and asked some of the tree spirits if they'd like to participate in an experiment. There were five trees, or groups of trees who agreed—the white pines, the fairy or yes tree, a big sycamore and some others. I set up an exercise where the workshop participants would walk around and spend some time being with each of those trees. I asked them what information they would intuitively receive about each tree. For instance, was the tree spirit male or female, what job does the tree do, and so on. I always picked up that the pine trees are very comforting, sweet natured trees, with a feminine presence. And that is the same notion that the workshop members, independently from both me and each other, got. People saw the mistletoe tree as masculine and that it grants wishes. I hadn't told anyone the story about the fairy lights, until after the first class.

Trees and I have always been good friends.

Sometimes the nature spirits look like sort of a heat shimmer, even when it is literally not a heat shimmer, not hot out and also at night. This year on May Eve I was by myself. One of my favorite plants growing up was honeysuckle. I had seen a little two inch tall fairy shape, but there was something different about the wings. On this night I went out with a question.

I had previously had a fairy guardian who showed up as a cloud shape. It happened on a day when I was having a tough time dealing with some human beings who were not being nice. When I looked up in the clouds I saw a very round faced fairy. She had a round body too, with little fairy wings. That was on April 1st so I called her April.

Now some guides can be with you for a long time and others for a shorter duration and you move on. So on May's Eve I wanted to know if April was still around or still a guide for me. This little figure showed up, not like the moving lights, several years ago in the yes tree, but like the emptiness at the middle of a little cobalt colored light—not a shadow. I got the intuitive feeling that the image of this spirit was my answer.

I asked, "What's your name?"

She said, "Let's go for a walk." The driveway loop is a tenth of a mile long, the same walk we use for the class. When I walked by one of our big honeysuckle bushes, I heard, "Look up!"

I looked at the tree and I saw that the shape of the honeysuckle flowers and leaves was the exact shape of the wings I had seen before.

Honeysuckle I thought. *That makes a lot of sense*, because I loved honeysuckle when I was growing up. Honeysuckle was my fairy godmother.

Don't Test the Fairies and other True Tales

Beth Wilder

On Halloween one year, my friend Mark and I were out back on Grand Avenue. We were standing amongst the trees at the back of the yard, where more of a spiritual presence could be felt. We looked in the crook of a tree and saw many tiny red lights swirling around. Mark wanted to put his hand there to see what would happen, and it seems I warned him he shouldn't disturb the fairies there. He did and immediately jerked his hand back. He said he felt a lot of prickles, and that it felt like a spider web was there. Fairies often play with people by making it feel like spider webs are brushing against them. When Mark got home, he had a rash on that arm that lasted for about 10 days. He figured he had tested the fairies a bit too far.

Pixabay photo fantasy-2824500_960_720

"The Raven"

In 1998, as I was walking along the sidewalk from my home to work, I was mesmerized by some vines in a tree near my house. The vines looked almost dead, although there were a few fresh leaves on them, but what was so eye-catching to me was the impression they gave of being something like a fancy apartment house for birds.

As I was gazing up at the vines, a bird darted right in front of me, and as it passed, I automatically turned to see what had just flown so close to me. When I turned, instead of a bird, I saw a tall man in a knee-length black coat, with his hands in his pockets. He had on a flat brimmed black hat, and his face was tilted down, so I could only really see a pale, pointed, "beaky" nose and chin. He had wispy, shoulder-length, champagne-colored hair. Surprisingly, I thought not a thing of it, as I continued on my way to work.

Later that day, my friend Mark had come to visit, and we were walking on the same sidewalk. We were in front of what I considered to be the most beautiful house on street, and I was looking at one of the enormous old trees in the yard, at the same pattern of vines, thinking the same thing I had earlier that day – how it looked like a fancy dwelling for birds or something. Just then, another bird darted in front of me. This time, when I turned around, I saw my friend Mark looking pale. Realizing he tends to lose color when he has "seen something not of this realm," I asked him what was wrong. He proceeded to tell me that as he turned to glance at the bird, he saw a man in a knee-length black coat, wearing a black hat, peering up at him.

Even though I had not yet mentioned to Mark what I had seen earlier that day, he proceeded to describe exactly what I had seen, with the only exceptions being that Mark beheld the man wearing a top hat, and he said the man's coat went to points in the back. We termed him "The Raven," since he seemed to be associated with a bird and was dressed all in black.

A few days after Mark and I saw "The Raven," in front of the same house where Mark saw it, a tree got struck by lightning and fell over. The tree that was hit looked the same as the one with the vines I had been looking at, but happened to be at the opposite corner of the lot near the sidewalk where Mark had seen "the Raven." We were very sad to lose that tree, as it seemed to mark the entrance to a more "magical" area of the street.

I picked up a few sherds of the lightning-struck wood, so I would have something to remember the tree. After I created a fetish for a friend out of some of the wood, a thunderstorm went through the area. As I lay in my bed, I smelled the wonderful perfume of burnt wood over my face, which has happened several times at night -- two times, in particular, I felt almost smothered, when I smelled this particular scent of burnt wood. It was then that heard the spirits ask me to write down what they had to say, which was the following:

When the Thunder Beings strike a tree, you shouldn't mourn for it, for it was chosen. It's like when someone lights sage or sweet grass, etc. – to purify, to smell the aroma and get peace & strength from it. That is what they are doing with the trees, and after all, are not trees to them like twigs would be to us? We would have no compunction about lighting something small to use ceremoniously.

As I wrote what I was given, I continued to smell the burnt wood fragrance, so I felt that was reinforcement of what the spirits were relating to me.

Sometime after the tree that had been struck by lightning was removed, the hole in the ground where it once stood was still evident. My Aunt Pat (who was somewhat psychic) came to visit, and we walked down the street so I could show her where the tree had fallen and she brought her camera along for some reason.

Just as we neared the hole in the ground, she excitedly said, "Oh, look! There is a big ball of light going up from the roots of the tree. I am going to get a picture of that!"

She snapped that photo, and then as she took a second picture of it, she said that she was not sure that she got all the orb in the frame on that one, as it was ascending higher right as she took the photo.

I have the two photos, and they do, indeed show just what she was describing to me. The first picture shows a huge ball of light that looks a lot like the sun, but the sun was not in that area of the sky at the time.

In the second photo, the ball of light has exited the frame, but the glow is still evident.

Upon closer inspection of the hole left in the ground by the tree roots, Aunt Pat said that it was a nexus, although she did not elaborate on that.

Scanned photos courtesy of Beth Wilder

The Redbud Tree

We had a darling Redbud tree in our backyard, and I loved to sit out on the swing and talk with it. One day, the tree Offered to let me "switch places" with it – that is, to let me see some of what it sees and feels. I happily agreed and closed my eyes. Almost immediately I saw bright, light green dappled movement and felt the most blissful, peaceful warmth and comfort I had ever experienced. Even sound seemed to be muted. Words cannot even begin to convey the utter serenity I felt for those few moments.

My Aunt Pat called the Redbud a "spirit tree," because it was filled with all kinds of shapes resembling faces and various animals. One day, I noticed a new "face" in the tree, just above a split near its roots. It looked like a sweet girl with braids on either side of her face, and she told me her name was Betsy. Then, just as she related that to me, two bumblebees flew all around me – it seemed quite intentional, as if they were saying, "The two B's (bees) – Beth and Betsy."

Sketch of Betsy the first day I "met" herArtwork with permission of Beth Wilder

Rain

One day, when I was sitting out on the front porch of my house, trying to hear what our gorgeous Japanese Magnolia and other trees had to say, I heard, "Pretty rain this evening." It had been cloudy, but no one held out hope for rain. A few minutes later, it began to thunder, then rain. It really poured. Mama came out front to tell me she was watching the weather channel and saw rain just appeared for us out of nowhere.

The Leafy Gnome

One day, I was at home alone, sitting in my huge platform rocking chair. All of a sudden, I felt something hit the back of the chair near my lower back – the force of the blow was enough to knock me forward, out of the chair.

I immediately got my bearings and ran around to the back of the chair to see what had hit it, and I saw running down the hallway, the back of a little brownish-green man – he couldn't have been even two feet tall. His little elbows were pumping fast as he ran, and he had on a little olive green cap and brownish pointed shoes – in fact, he looked completely a dark olive green, and leaves were sticking out all over him.

As he reached the closed closet door at the end of the hall, he just disappeared into it. I think he was just having fun with me.

Leafy Gnome artwork and permission
Beth Wilder

The Earth Deva on Taylorsville Lake Road

In 2011, driving to work, I was praying and thanking God for the beautiful day. I don't think I'd even crossed the county line, when I was kind of looking off to the land to my right on Taylorsville Lake Road, praying God to take care of Mother Earth.

I was caught totally by surprise when ahead of me on the road (maybe 15-20 yards or so), I saw a huge, lovely woman's head rising out of the road. It blended in with the surroundings, so it looked rather ghostly, but I am sure I saw it, because it was so unexpected and sudden.

She only appeared from the shoulders up and looked greyish (because of the road), but she was serene and beautiful, and it's like she was lifting her head up out of the earth. She had to be very tall -- her head seemed as large as the trees on the side of the road, and they were very tall.

It was quite a glorious blessing, and I am so grateful she showed herself to me.

Beautiful Earth Goddess artwork and permission courtesy
Beth Wilder

Beth Wilder, is author and illustrator of The Twilight Realm: A Tarot
of Faery

A Few Other Wood Working Artists

Betty Buehler:

Wood speaks. Whether cedar, cottonwood bark, cypress knee, or other found wood, each piece has a hidden figure inside! The mystique of carving these types of wood is to release what is awaiting discovery, be it a tree, a gnome, a Santa, or my favorite—a dwelling.

I began carving about 11 years ago, with the help of books, trial and error, and a famous bark carver, Rick Jensen. Cottonwood bark is my preferred medium and it is a fallen wood. I scavenge a lot of material along the banks of the Ohio River, all of which is from fallen wood. My pieces are primarily hand-carved, keeping power carving to a minimum. Betty Buehler, Louisville, KY
For commission inquiries and more information about Betty's artwork, contact her at gajessimo@gmail.com.

Little house by Betty Buehler, artist
Photo courtesy of Betty Buehler

Lindsay Frost:

All of my woodworking is done with 'found wood', meaning it has fallen due to nature or man, but not me. I take the found wood and give it a new life, transforming it into a piece of beauty that will again delight man. Wood is older than mankind and has a story to tell us and its own energy. The story is in the grain, the rhythm of the flow, be it a slow or a dynamic grain. The grain moves around where a limb was, or where lightning struck and burned the tree. Wood is always trying to heal itself, just as man does. But sometimes the wound is too deep, or the disease too severe. Does this sound like a living entity?

Each of my containers tells a tale, of the struggles in growth, success in reaching the sun, imperfections from lightning and insects, drought and fire. This is what makes each individual container unique. Wood has a calming effect on humans. Have you ever caught yourself unconsciously rubbing a piece of wood? It doesn't have to be a decorative piece, or a carved piece. You look down on the ground and see an unusually shaped twig, and you pick it up. You hold it in your hand and walk off. And it's still in your hand. What is happening here? I don't need to tell you what is happening. Ask your conscious mind, if you dare.

Michelangelo said that every block of marble contained a figure, and it was his job to remove the excess marble and release the figure within. It is my job to remove the excess wood and release the spirit in the wood to please man. Then the Dryads will smile.

Namaste: The spirit within me bows to the spirit within you.

Contact Lindsay E. Frost at lindsayefrost.com

Wild Cherry Burl 2017, Art and photo courtesy Lindsay Frost

Notes and Final Commentary

Lightning struck wood in Chinese lore is regarded as good for expelling ghosts and malevolent spirits. Also, a piece of wood that has been struck by lightning is believed to be a most powerful talisman. It is empowered by Divine forces, and is protection against all harm. Thor, the Norse God of Thunder, was once believed to have hallowed wood by hitting it with lightning.

Powder Post Beetle Wood boring beetles most often attack dying or dead trees. In forest settings, they are important in the turnover of trees by culling weak trees, thus allowing new growth to occur. Wood bored holes are a symbol of culling your own weaknesses, so only your strengths come through the wand. (Courtesy Beth Wilder, Louisville, Kentucky)

Which meaning is valid? Remember that, since trees and woods offer us so much in a multiple layering of benefits, you can find tree information that is botanical, folklore, practical, and also knowledge connected to Earth-based spirituality or metaphysical lineage. Many and separate parts of the tree will contribute to our health and well-being, including tree flowers, essential oils, bark, roots, fruit and nuts, lumber and of course there are environmental benefits such as holding and improving soil and giving us oxygen to breathe—removing carbon dioxide.

As there are different sources and information that can be complementary not repetitive, one must choose which description best matches what they feel or for which they are oriented to use the wood and wand. For example, let's pick one wood out of the lot in which to compare the differing meanings—black walnut. I chose this wood as there are meanings in very divergent directions, most likely stemming from very different lineages of knowledge.

Here are the meanings for Black walnut from ten sources: 1. Friendly, positive, helps underdog, 2. Strength, haven for nature spirits, 3. Helps us to lighten up and find humor, 4. Linked with love and romance and divination for same, wards off lightning, 5. Opens us to new perspectives, has knowledge of the mysteries of death and rebirth, doorway into the faerie realm that can initiate change, draws and houses faeries, 6. Protection against sickness or pregnancy, contains power to harm if necessary, 7. Good for weather magic, attuned to the crown chakra—ability to open to the fullest dimension of being, good for spells of teleportation astral travel and inspiration, 8. Change, link breaker, menopause, puberty, moving, let go of the past, protection from outside influences and energies, helps you adjust to major changes, 9. A thoughtful and serious wood, geared toward introspection and assists with inner clarity, 10. Couples reason with intuition to help a person grow spiritually and to heal from within, it is a quiet, unassuming wood, helps us to get in touch with ourselves and the Earth.

Trees and woods keep giving us in terms of materials and energetic vibrations, even long after they are buried under earth or ocean. Three examples of wood that has been altered via time and geological processes include bog wood, jet and petrified wood—all which are made into beautiful art.

Raw black jet and pendants crafted from jet
Artwork and photo by Thomas Freese

Within our modern, and ancient, knowledge of multi-determinate reality and string theory, we can say for sure that there are likely unlimited meanings for just one tree and wood. If you obtain a black walnut wand, then you may relate to some, or all of these meanings and you may well find other unique uses for a black walnut wand— connections not mentioned above. Or, you may explore just one of the meanings noted above, such as the connection with the faerie realm. Follow your intuition, your spirit guidance for how best to use your wand.

Summary

"I frequently tramped eight or ten miles through the deepest snow to keep an appointment with a beech-tree, or a yellow birch, or an old acquaintance among the pines."
Henry David Thoreau

In summary, how does one decide which wand, or what set of wands, will be the best for psychic protection? Or which wood to keep close in a pendant or to use every day for a spoon or other crafted object. That depends on which tree/wood/wand you relate to, are connected with, have a history of communication. If you want to bring in angelic protection, I would suggest you check out a hemlock wand. If you are taking up the fight to protect others, then holly would be an excellent choice. Perhaps if you have a tricky entity and you'd like to bring in a team of helpful and protective spirits, then black locust could be a wise choice. If the energies around you that are intrusive have run down your immune system, then maybe willow would be a good option. I have seen a number of folks reach for the lightning struck Sequoia when they want to regain balance and let the power of the Universe flow from their feet upward, like the giant redwood. Mahogany can help you overcome fears and negative emotions that may have found a temporary home within you—and once those fears and troublesome energies within you are released, then the difficult entities will find they cannot coexist in your home and around you—no matter where you go. Maple takes a stand for your protection, very simply put. Others may find a refuge in woods that connect more with healing, and from that experience, they find they are protected, and there are many woods available that focus on

177

healing—such as purpleheart, African Blackwood, Pink ivory, cherry and hemlock.

I keep the whole armamentarium of some 70 woods, ready to gift or sell to those who touch the essence of a particular tree and know within their heart, mind and soul, that wood is there to help them—NOW!

Please feel free to contact the gifted and professional psychic readers who provided the channeled information above on the metaphysical meaning of the woods and trees. They are listed below with a very brief biography. For all three, this was not their usual work but they willingly agreed to the experiment.

Feel free to contact me, Thomas Freese, for consultations about wand workshops and wands that I have made for sale or which I could custom make for you—I wood-burn special symbols for protection on wands, such as Celtic knots.

Professional Psychic Contributors

I sent out numbered wood samples, totaling 71 kinds of trees/woods. Each sample had only a number for identification, and the psychic contributors had no idea from which tree each wood sample was. Only one of the three psychics had possession, over time, of all 71 woods, due to the logistics and conveniences of distance and time.

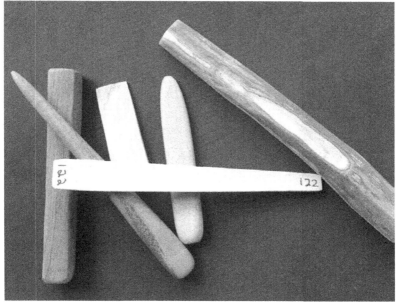

A few numbered wood samples, photo by Thomas Freese

Wood meanings noted above that do not have the initials (as above, LB, AC and DE, of the psychics who channeled information), are provided with permission from two online sources:

1. Kate Raymond. Kate is an artist with lovely wands, pendants and other items in The Original Natural Wood Wand Shop on Etsy. Kate says, "I live in the far south of the UK, a mile from the coast roughly half way between Dartmouth and Plymouth. I make traditional magical tools out of native British woods, trying as much as possible to follow the methods our ancestors would have used. The wood I use is locally grown and ethically sourced, I do all the work by hand without any power tools and I use an organic, non-toxic oil to help bring out the natural beauty and preserve the wood." Contact her through Etsy.

2. Fey Wilde and Gina Salvatoriello, co-creators of the information found on Project Fey, Website: www.ProjectFey.com.

LB Laura Berlin

Laura is a psychic and her website is www.asklaura.org. Laura says, "I've known since the age of four that I was different but I didn't know why. I could see things which others couldn't, but my family didn't want to believe me. In my late 30's I realized these visions were connections to spirits from the other side. This realization saved my life and led me to the path of guiding and assisting others in their spiritual journey."

Laura has a unique way of doing readings. She is descriptive and concise with her visions. Her goal is to guide her clients for success in their everyday life. "I will continue doing psychic readings because this is what I truly love. My clients come from all over the world. They're looking for a psychic medium or a psychic online to provide them peace of mind, a feeling of security or success."

Laura Berlin photo and notes from wood samples, both courtesy of
Laura Berlin

AC Angie Clark

Angie is an international psychic, energy healer, channel, medium, exorcist, master teacher and spiritual guide. Angie has been a sensitive all her life and works continuously to hone her skills and connect to Spirit. She derives her information through her senses. Her primary methods are claircognizance (knowing), clairvoyance (seeing) and clairsentience (feeling).

Angie has crafted her own brand of energy healing. It is a blend of guided meditation, chakra/meridian balancing, energy cleansing, psychic reading and rebalancing. Each session is channeled and unique.

Angie reads like a psychic life coach and works with premonition. In addition, she accesses Akashic records to help you not only know what your future hold but to help you unlock your potential to create the future you wish to live. She also has a unique ability to help you see situations from a different perspective and how to heal the past energetically.

Her website is www.Angieclarkhealer.com.

Angie Clark, photo courtesy of
Angie Clark

DE Dale Epley

I was a 'late bloomer'… already in my 40s before my interest in the metaphysical began. Originally, all I wanted to do was to learn to find the peace that I had heard meditation could help with. But soon learned there was so much more to be gained. As I proceeded with meditation, reading, and metaphysical classes including many different healing modalities, I found a 'me' that felt right.

I progressed quickly in my interest of channeling and psychic development, but felt there was so much more available than even the 'new' me had touched on. In my excitement to learn all I could about my 'people' in Spirit, I found new clarity in the person that I am, as well as learning that I am not alone in my endeavors here on earth… I (and you) have a whole regiment of help in the Spirit world dedicated to helping us as much as we allow.

This journey has taken me from Texas to Kentucky and now to Tennessee and along the way we've experienced many adventures. Some of the more exciting ones were traveling all over the United States to work at many different Psychic fairs, meeting many different people of all walks of life. We have created a website (www.angelspeak.net), many meditations on CD for myself and our public, a book with my Joy Guide, Daisy ("Daisy, My Life as a Joy Guide") which gives some great information on how to learn about and work with your Joy Guide and Angels.

And now, at 70, I'm ready to see where this next chapter in my life takes me.

Dale's website is www.angelspeak.net and her contact phone number is 865-484-1391.

Dale Epley photo courtesy of
Dale Epley

185

Bibliography and Recommended Books

Andrews, Ted. *Enchantment of the Faerie Realm: Communicate with Nature Spirits and Elementals.* St. Paul, MN: Llewellyn Publications, 1993.

Constantine, Albert Jr. *Know Your Woods: A Complete Guide to Trees, Woods, and Veneers*, Revised Edition. New York: Charles Scribner's Sons, 1975.

Domine, David. *True Ghost Stories and Eerie Legends from America's Most Haunted Neighborhood.* Charleston, SC: CreateSpace Independent Publishing Platform, 2014.

Fraser, Sir James George. *The Golden Bough: A Study in Magic and Religion: A New Abridgement from the Second and Third Editions (Oxford World's Classics).* Oxford: Oxford University Press, 2009.

Hageneder, Fred. *The Meaning of Trees: Botany, History, Healing, Lore.* San Francisco: Chronicle Books, 2005.

Hugo, Nancy Ross. *Trees Up Close: The Beauty of bark, leaves, flowers, and seeds.* Portland, Oregon: Timber Press, 2014.

Little, Elbert L. *National Audubon Society Field Guide to Trees, Eastern Region.* New York: Knopf, 1980.

MacLir, Alferian Gwydion. *Wandlore: The Art of Crafting the Ultimate Magical Tool.* Woodbury, MN: Llewellyn Publications, 2011.

Meier, Eric. *Fluorescence: A Secret Weapon in Wood Identification.* The Wood Database: http://www.wood-database.com/wood-articles/fluorescence-a-secret-weapon-in-wood-identification/

Moon, Beth. *Ancient Trees: Portraits of Time.* New York: Abbeville Press, 2014.

Murray, Liz and Colin. *The Celtic Tree Oracle: A System of Divination.* New York: St. Martin's Press, 1988.

Pickering, David. *Cassell's Dictionary of Superstitions.* London: Cassell, 2002.

Salvatoriello, Gina & Wilde, Fey. *The Magickal Properties of Wood.* August 16, 2013. Project Fey: http://www.wood-database.com/wood-articles/fluorescence-a-secret-weapon-in-wood-identification/

Silverstein, Shel. *The Giving Tree.* New York: Harper Collins, 1999.

Stael von Holstein, Verena. *Nature Spirits and What They Say.* Glasgow: Floris Books, 2003.

Stael von Holstein, Verena. *Nature Spirits of the Trees.* Glasgow: Floris Books, 2009.

Struthers, Jane. *The Wisdom of Trees Oracle: 40 Oracle Cards for Wisdom and Guidance.* London: Watkins Publishing, 2012.

Teague, Gypsey Elaine. *The Witch's Guide to Wands.* San Francisco: Red Wheeler/Weiser, 2015.

The Findhorn Community. *The Findhorn Garden.* New York: Harper and Row, 1975.

Tomkins, Peter & Bird, Christopher. *The Secret Life of Plants: A Fascinating Account of the Physical, Emotional, and Spiritual Relations Between Plants and Man.* New York: Harper Collins, 1973.

Wohlleben, Peter. *The Hidden Life of Trees: What They Feel, How They Communicate—Discoveries from a Secret World.* Vancouver: Greystone Books, 2016.

Comparisons for the meanings of black walnut—sources listed with numbers:
1. Laura Berlin, 2. Dale Epley, 3. Angie Small, 4. Cassell's Dictionary of Superstitions, 5. Ted Andrews, 6. Gypsey Teague, 7. Wandlore by Maclir, 8. Bach Flower Essences, 9. McTaggert's Woods (http://mctaggertswoods.com/maprofwo.html), 10. GoldenTree Wands (http://api.ning.com/files/aIdTp6ti391mwgmRVKvp4dhU*PNXAaspGwmxdCO-xwaOBBzVFtH7qEPpPiZsfen1vuDlEkVmdDYMt*UjLxo4WgFniJCQtqJu/magicalpropertiesofwood.pdf).

Mickie Mueller's story on a blog post:
http://mickiemuellerart.blogspot.com/2014/11/wild-persimmons-after-first-frost.html

Notes for the photo of farmer dowsing:
https://en.wikipedia.org/wiki/Dowsing

Picture caption: 1942: George Casely uses a hazel twig to attempt to find water on the land around his Devon farm

"This photograph was scanned and released by the Imperial War Museum on the IWM Non Commercial Licence. The image was catalogued by the IWM as created for the Ministry of Information, which was dissolved in 1946. Consequently, the image and faithful reproductions are considered Crown Copyright, now expired as the photograph was taken prior to 1 June 1957."

About the Author

Thomas Freese performing stories with grade school children

Thomas Lee Freese is an author, artist, intuitive, teaching artist and storyteller. He has written 12 books and has a set of audio books/performances. Thomas has written 200 articles and reviews, including ten years of monthly travel articles for Lexington's Southsider Magazine. He is a juried Roster Artist with the Kentucky Arts Council Teaching Artists and a member of the Kentucky Storytelling Association. His website is www.ThomasLFreese.com.

Thomas Freese has a wide range of wood crafts, including wands, spoons, ornaments, wall carvings, beads, pins, pendants, earrings and chakra sticks. He also works in bone, stone, shell and antler.

Catlinite fox fetish and photo by Thomas Freese

Thomas is a teaching artist and has worked since 1994 as an artist in residence in schools, libraries and also doing workshops in visual arts and storytelling. He is a member of the Louisville Artisans Guild and sells at area crafts events. In addition, Thomas Freese works with the Kentucky Center for the Arts, Arts in Healing program, storytelling and teaching art in assisted living, veterans' facilities, children's homes and other venues.

As a storyteller, Thomas has been on tour in Argentina, and he has over 20 educational and entertaining story programs. He plays guitar, harmonica and other musical instruments and performs for all ages or mixed aged audiences; in homes, churches, events, corporate settings, schools, libraries and more. As a professional speaker, he has a wide range of programs. He has bilingual story programs, combining English and Spanish.

Thomas Lee Freese has a BA in Psychology, and a Master's Degree in Expressive Therapies. He is a Licensed Professional Clinical Counselor (LPCC) and a Board Certified and Registered Art Therapist (ATR-BC). His books include:

Shaker Ghost Stories from Pleasant Hill, Kentucky
Fog Swirler and 11 Other Ghost Stories
Strange and Wonderful Things: A Collection of Ghost
Stories with Special Appearances by
        Witches and Other Bizarre Creatures
Making Wood Jewelry Southwest Style
Haunted Battlefields of the South
Ghosts, Spirits and Angels: True Tales from Kentucky and
Beyond
More True Tales of Ghosts, Spirits and Angels
Halloween Sleepwalker
Shaker Spirits, Shaker Ghosts
Eerie Encounters in Everyday Life: Angels, Aliens,
Ghosts, Haunts
Tree Spirits, Wood Wisdom

Soon to be released through Stellium Books!

The King Determined to Die
By Thomas Lee Freese

This rhyming narrative is a poignant parable for our times. It is for children and grownups both, and features the perceptive artwork of Jill Baker. Thomas Freese has read this story in schools, and children are fascinated at the dynamic interplay of a bitter king and an innocent child. It is a redemptive tale that may well mirror today's corruption and greed...although written in 1998.

Illustration by Beth Wilder, scanned with permission

Made in the USA
Monee, IL
11 July 2020